ATTACK ON PEARL HARBOR

December 7, 1941

Tonight - at 6 oc P.M. I sit here by lantern light inside the telephone exchange. Today - will go down in history. I am alone. ~~My~~ men have gone to the fields anywhere - to get away The place has been bombed terribly. We were caught completely by surprise. Our planes were 60% burned. This barracks

Battleship Row as depicted by a Japanese artist on a post card issued by the Imperial Japanese Navy Supply Office.

ATTACK ON PEARL HARBOR

A PICTORIAL HISTORY

STAN COHEN

LIBRARY OF CONGRESS
CONTROL NUMBER 81-83760

ISBN 1-57510-087-8

First Printing: April 2001

This book is also titled, *East Wind Rain, A Pictorial History
of the Pearl Harbor Attack,* first printed 1981.

Cover Artwork: Mel Brown, Austin, Texas
Typography: Arrow Graphics, Missoula, Montana

PICTORIAL HISTORIES PUBLISHING COMPANY, INC.
713 South Third Street West, Missoula, Montana 59801
Phone (406) 549-8488 FAX (406) 728-9280
E-Mail—phpc@montana.com
Website—pictorialhistoriespublishing.com

Introduction

*I*ndividual events can change the course of history. During the moments, minutes or hours in which the outcome of such an event is still uncertain, the world's future can hang in the balance. Certainly American history was in limbo when the 'shot heard round the world' was fired at Lexington, when South Carolinians fired on Fort Sumter, when Presidents Lincoln and Kennedy were shot down and when Black Tuesday heralded the 1929 stock market crash.

The two-hour attack on Pearl Harbor, Hawaii, on Sunday morning, Dec. 7, 1941, ranks among those remarkable moments that changed not only American history but events in the rest of the world. One could say that from the time the Japanese planes left their carriers until the first bomb dropped at 7:55 a.m., the world was in limbo. It is easy to sit back 50 years later and second-guess the actions of those who took part in this momentous event, and to speculate about the "what ifs." What if the Japanese had made a third attack and knocked out the fleet's fuel tanks or shipyard facilities, forcing all U.S. ships back to California? What if intelligence from Washington had resulted in a full-scale military alert in Hawaii before the attack? What if the Japanese fleet had been spotted at sea before December 7, or if radar contacts of the incoming enemy planes had been interpreted and reported effectively?

The events leading up to the December 7 attack will probably always be clouded in controversy. Some historians have suggested that President Roosevelt knew about the attack in advance or virtually provoked an attack in the belief that such a shock would be the only way that the American people could be coaxed into the war against the Axis powers. There has not been any evidence which points to that hypothesis, but his motivations and intentions remain one of history's secrets. The Pearl Harbor attack is the subject of dozens of books, both pictorial and narrative. I have not tried to uncover' anything new, but to present the most comprehensive collection of pictures of the historic event that has yet been done. Recently visiting the sites of military bases that were attacked, I snapped pictures from the vantage points of the photographers who took the spectacular December 7 photos included in this book. It was like stepping back in time, and it was not hard to imagine the sound of exploding bombs and machine gun fire, and to see the sky filled with oily smoke.

If you are old enough to remember Pearl Harbor or were actually there, return now to that Sunday morning and relive those stunning, world-shaking moments. If you are too young to remember, I hope that as this pictorial history unfolds before you, you can better understand what happened and how those few hours changed the course of history.

50th Anniversary Introduction

It has been 10 years since the introduction of this book. Thousands of copies have been sold throughout the world. It has been extremely gratifying to see that one of the most towering events in American history still captures the interest of people.

In the past 10 years, much new material about the attack has surfaced, along with many new photographs. Corrected revisions along with new material abound in this 10th anniversary edition, which is fittingly published on the 50th anniversary of the attack.

Much has happened in the 50 years since Dec. 7, 1941. Our enemies are now our friends, and even one of our friends (the USSR)—which became our enemy—is now friendly again. The world order has changed considerably. While America is undoubtedly the world's military power, Japan has risen to the forefront as an economic force. As a result, the Japanese have purchased much of Hawaii and own a considerable stake in business throughout the United States proper.

How history has come full circle in the past five decades.

I hope this expanded and revised *East Wind Rain* will stand as the definitive photo history of the event. Also hopefully this edition will serve as a learning tool for younger generations and a nostalgic trip for the generations old enough to remember.

—Stan Cohen

Acknowledgments

The following people provided assistance in the preparation of the first edition of this book in 1981: R.H. Rothrock and Lt. Cmdr. Art Humphries, Pearl Harbor Naval Base Public Affairs Office; Gary Beito, Arizona Memorial Museum Association; Gary Cummins and staff, Arizona Memorial, National Park Service; Dorothy Fuller, Naval Base Library; Kaye Jordan, Wing Historian, Hickam AFB; Maj. Dan Arnold, Wheeler AFB; Sgt. Jack Lowney and Capt. Glenn Exum, PAO, Schofield Barracks; John Fairbank, PAO, Pearl Harbor Naval Shipyard; John Burlage, PAO, U.S. Pacific Fleet; Dennis Fujii and Staff Sgt. Laura Murphy, PAO, Hickam AFB; Will Kranz, PAO, U.S. Army, Ft. Shafter; Capt. Bill Wood, PAO, Kaneohe MCAS; Lt. Cmdr. Joe Herrell and Warrant Officer Robert Geihl, PAO, Barbers Point NAS; JOC Cindy Adams, PAO, Submarine Base, Pearl Harbor; Tom Fairfull, U.S. Army Museum Hawaii; and Werner Stoy, Camera Hawaii, Honolulu.

This revised edition could not have been completed without the able assistance of Ernest Arroyo and Robert Bracci, who reworked most of the captions, provided many new photos and gave editorial advice; David Aiken, who supplied much new material on the attack's aerial episodes; Paul Bender, who provided the aircraft profiles and original drawings; Ray Emory, a Pearl Harbor survivor, who furnished much new technical data; Mel Brown with his new cover artwork; and Al Makiel, who has supplied information and photos for many years; and to the following members of the Pearl Harbor History Associates: Robert Varrill, Jesse Pond Jr., Gene Camp, John DiVirgillio and William Cleveland.

The Hawaiian connection was essential to the completion of this new volume. In particular, Dan Martinez, chief historian at the Arizona Memorial; Bob Chenoweth, curator at the Memorial; and Burl Burlingame, reporter for the *Honolulu Star-Bulletin*.

In addition, I wish to thank Bob Cressman and Bob Sumrall for providing new photos; John Lambert, Harry Brown and Lee Embree for new aerial activity photos and information; Skip Rains for some new stories; Otto Lang; and Dr. Martin Davis. The staff of the Admiral Nimitz Museum; the Intrepid Sea-Air-Space Museum; and Patriots Point Naval and Maritime Museum provided photographs. Daniel Lenihan of the Submerged Cultural Resources Unit of the National Park Service provided photos and drawings of the sunken *Arizona* and *Utah*.

And finally, much thanks to the Pearl Harbor Survivors Association, and especially Ed Chappell, who have allowed me to attend their national conventions for the past 10 years and interview hundreds of survivors.

Charles Hood of the University of Montana Journalism School edited the original manuscript and Chris Harris proofread the revised copy. Bruce Donnelly produced the maps and Dick Guth and Leslie Over keyboarded the revisions. Arrow Graphics typeset the revised edition.

Photo Credits

Photographs for this book were obtained from many sources. The following abbreviations have been used with negative numbers, where possible:

NA—National Archives
USN—United States Navy Archives
USA—United States Army Archives
USMC—United States Marine Corps Archives
HA—Hawaii State Archives
AMC—Arizona Memorial Collection
EA—Ernest Arroyo Collection
AM—Al Makiel Collection
UH—University of Hawaii Archives

Photos not credited were taken by the author or are from his collection. Other sources are acknowledged.

Contents

This June 14, 1941, issue of *Collier's* Magazine had a long article on the defenses of Pearl Harbor. Six months later the Japanese would make a mockery of "Impregnable Pearl Harbor."

IMPREGNABLE PEARL HARBOR
By Walter Davenport

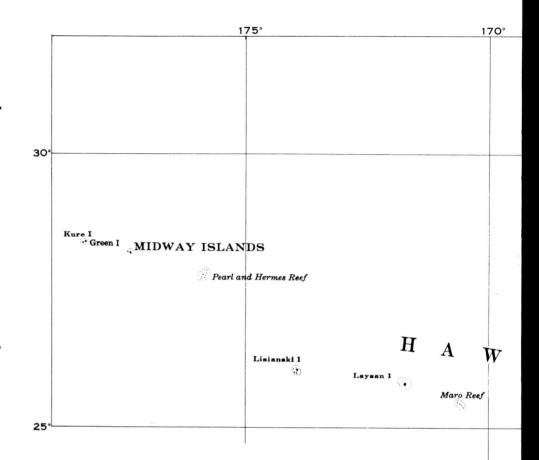

"On the day of Pearl Harbor, America's slowly rising interest in the troubles of Great Britain crystallized instantly into an understanding of dangers confronting America. On that day, Dec. 7, 1941, the words 'Pearl Harbor' took on a meaning of time, formerly they meant only a place. Now we say, 'before Pearl Harbor,' or 'after Pearl Harbor.' America thinks of 'Pearl Harbor' as the day of her great decisions." William R. Furlong

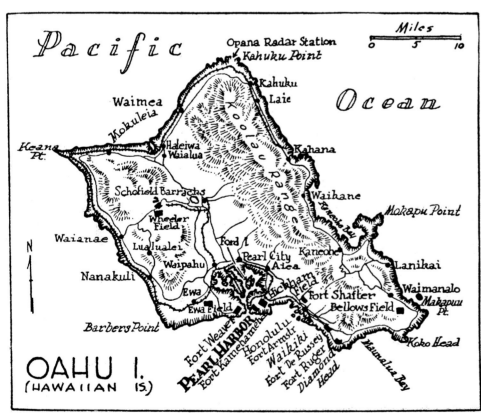

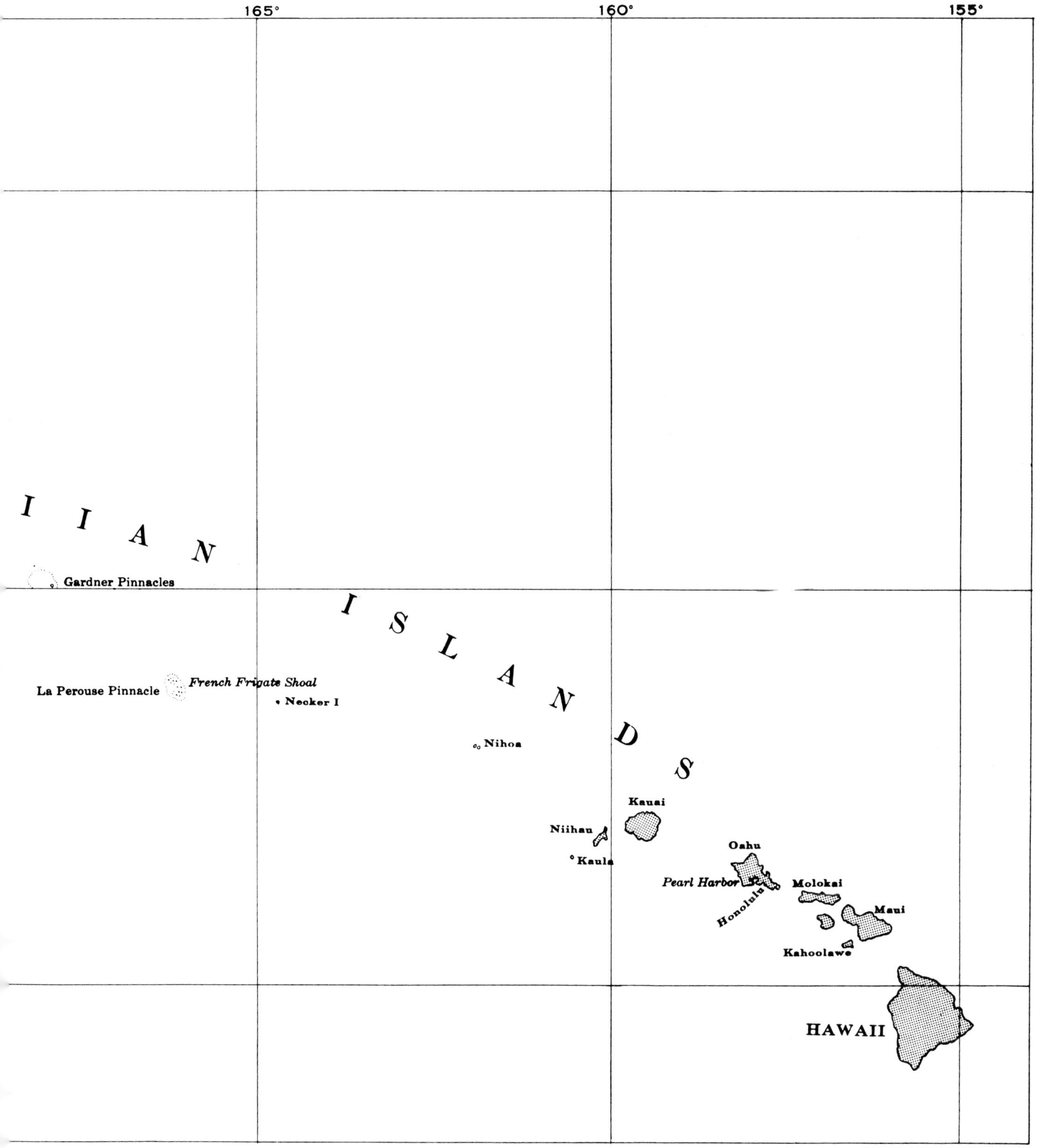

I I A N

Gardner Pinnacles

I S L A N D S

La Perouse Pinnacle · French Frigate Shoal
· Necker I

·· Nihoa

Kauai

Niihau
° Kaula

Oahu

Pearl Harbor

Molokai

Honolulu

Maui

Kahoolawe

HAWAII

165°   160°   155°

Remember
Pearl Harbor

14

The Oregonian

ESTABLISHED BY HENRY L. PITTOCK
An Independent Republican Newspaper
Published Daily, Except Sunday, by The Oregonian
Publishing Company, Oregonian Bldg., 537 S. W. Sixth
Ave., Portland, Oregon. Telephone AT 2121.
Sole ownership of The Oregonian resides in the
H. L. Pittock Family and the Scott Company

CAROLINE P. LEADBETTER,   PALMER HOYT,
President   Publisher

The Oregonian is a member of the Associated Press.
The Associated Press is exclusively entitled to the use
for publication of all news dispatches credited to it or
not otherwise credited in this paper, and also the local
news published herein. All rights of publication of special dispatches herein are also reserved.

National Advertising Offices—Paul Block and Associates, 400 Madison ave., New York city; 919 N. Mich-
igan ave., Chicago; General Motors bldg., Detroit; 1420
Walnut, Philadelphia; Monadnock bldg., San Francisco; Chamber of Commerce bldg., Los Angeles; 1411
Fourth Avenue bldg., Seattle; Little bldg., Boston.

DECEMBER 10, 1941

Remember Pearl Harbor!

The reactions of the American citizen of the
Pacific coast to the opening of war with Japan
are not different from those of his fellow citizen in another part of the country, except that

Background
Rising Sun Over the Pacific

The Pacific Fleet sometimes anchored at Lahaina on the west coast of Maui as this photo shows. Just before the attack, the Japanese launched a float plane from the cruiser *Tone*, to make the sure the *Anchorage* was empty, thus confirming their intelligence that the fleet was at Pearl Harbor. USN

Japan's aggressive tendencies had shown themselves much earlier, when without warning, she had attacked China in 1895 and the Russians in the Far East in 1904. The victories contributed to the notion among some Japanese that Nippon could—and should—expand her territory and influence to other parts of the Pacific.

With limited land and natural resources and an expanding population, Japan inevitably looked beyond her borders to find solutions to her problems. Under the aegis of the Greater East Asia Co-Prosperity Sphere, she expanded her interests in the Pacific, milking anti-colonialist sentiment by advocating "Asia for the Asians." She was also strengthening her army and navy. In 1931, Japan invaded Manchuria and set up a puppet government. Though she had signed the 1922 Washington Naval Treaty, which limited the size of the British, American and Japanese navies, she renounced the agreement in 1936 and built up her navy until it had reached parity with those of Britain and the U.S.

The United States had historically been committed to maintaining China's independence, and when Japanese troops in Manchuria invaded China proper in July 1937, the seemingly inevitable slide toward an armed conflict between America and Japan began.

In Europe, Germany and Italy were paralleling Japan's aggressiveness. The United States was increasingly torn between conflicting notions: the impulse toward her isolationist traditions, and, on the other hand, the desire to help friendly nations who were being gobbled up by aggressors.

On Nov. 25, 1936, Germany and Japan signed their Anti-Comintern Pact. Italy joined them in 1937. In September 1940, Japan signed a treaty of alliance with Germany and Italy, which assured each country mutual assistance in time of war and set up spheres of influence for each country.

The world finally went to war in September 1939. With the fall of France in 1940, Japan occupied part of French Indo-China and eyed the rich natural resources of Thailand, Malaya and the Dutch East Indies.

As Japan continued to press its militaristic policies, the relations between that country and the United States deteriorated rapidly. In April 1940, the U.S. fleet sailed for maneuvers in the Hawaiian area. A month later, President Roosevelt ordered that the fleet be stationed in Hawaii indefinitely as a deterrent to further Japanese expansion in Asia. In July 1940, Roosevelt invoked the Export Control Act, prohibiting the export of strategic minerals and equipment and the flow of oil, scrap iron and steel to Japan.

When the oil embargo was imposed, Japan had a reserve of more than six million tons, which with strict economy would last three to four years. Without oil, Japan would have to bow to the will of the Allied powers. This she would not do. She needed the oil of Southeast Asia.

By 1939, powerful Japanese officials were dedicated to a policy of war. In October 1941, the conservative members in the Japanese government, including Premier Konoye, were forced to resign. The hawkish army faction gained control, and established Gen. Hideki Tojo as the new premier.

Adm. Harold Stark, chief of naval operations at the time of the attack. USN NH 61815

The United States of the early 1940s also was gearing up for war. In August 1940, the National Guard was mustered into federal service. In September, 50 U.S.-built destroyers were transferred to Great Britain, and in the same month, the first peacetime conscription law was enacted. In March 1941, the Lend-Lease Act was signed into law, making the United States for all intents and purposes a belligerent without having decalred war. All Japanese, German and Italian assets in the United States were frozen in June and July. About the same time, Lend-Lease was extended to Russia in June after she was attacked by Germany. An August 1941 meeting between Roosevelt and Prime Minister Churchill of Great Britain produced the Atlantic Charter, which stated the aims of the two countries regarding a future world order.

On Sept. 3, 1941, the United States asked Japan to accept the following four principles as a basis for any further discussions: (1) respect for the territorial integrity and sovereignty of all nations; (2) noninterference in the internal affairs of other nations; (3) equality of opportunity in trade and economic matters; (4) status quo throughout the Pacific area. In October, the U.S. requested that Japan withdraw from China and Indo-China.

Of course, Japan had no intention of bowing to these American demands. Already planning the surprise attack on Pearl Harbor, she continued to take part in diplomatic negotiations with America.

Special ambassador Saburo Kurusu joined Kichisaburo Nomura, the Japanese ambassador in Washington, to take part in the increasingly strained negotiations with the U.S.

A Japanese inspection party
at the 1933 Gymkana
(horse and transportation
show) at Schofield Barracks.
COURTESY LYMAN WOODMAN

Officers of the Navy's Hawaiian detachment with army officers at Hawaiian Department Headquarters in 1940.
Front row from left are Rear Adm. J. H. Newton, Rear Adm. R. E. Ingersoll, Vice Adm. A. Andrews, Maj. Gen.
Heron and Rear Adm. R. S. Holmes. Middle row: Lt. Comdr. Bell, Capt. T. S. Wilkinson and an unidentified ar-
my officer. Top row: unidentified Army and Navy officers, Lt. Flynn. USN

Cordell Hull, Secretary of State from 1933 to 1944, led the negotiations with the Japanese during the months leading up to the Pearl Harbor attack. NA

Joseph Grew, United States ambassador to Japan, 1932-1941. Interned in Japan after Pearl Harbor, he was exchanged in 1942 for Japanese diplomats. USN

They presented what would become Japan's final set of proposals on Nov. 20, 1941.

Secretary of State Cordell Hull countered on Nov. 26 with proposals that he knew would not be accepted. They called for Japan to withdraw from all the territories she had conquered by military on diplomatic means. While Hull's proposals were being studied in Tokyo, the Japanese fleet was steaming toward Hawaii.

Meanwhile, U.S. cryptographers, with the aid of a remarkable machine, had broken Japan's Purple Code, thus giving American officials access to secret Japanese diplomatic cables. Code-named "Magic," the information obtained from the decoded Japanese dispatches was enormously valuable to the American government. However, the date and place of the planned attack on the U.S. apparently were not transmitted to Washington.

The last days of November and the first week of December 1941 were critical to both sides. On November 30, Tojo rejected the final American proposals, and on December 2 the U.S. intercepted an encoded Japanese message directing all diplomatic and consular posts to destroy codes and ciphers and to burn confidential and secret material. The consulate in Honolulu was ordered to continue to send reports of ship movements at Pearl Harbor, a task it had been performing in secret for some time.

The "winds" messages, announcing its military intentions were broadcast to Japanese diplomats throughout the world. One of these—"East Wind Rain"—was the code phrase for war with the United States.

At 1 p.m. Washington time on December 7, the two Japanese ambassadors in the American capital were to present Secretary Hull a note stating that negotiations were broken off and that a state of war existed between the two nations.

To achieve technical compliance with international rules of war, the message was to be delivered about one half hour before Japanese planes struck Pearl Harbor, but owing to decoding difficulties at the Japanese embassy the note was not delivered until after hostilities had begun. Apparently the two ambassadors had not been informed of the surprise attack plans in advance.

During recent months the United States had been beefing up her military strength in Hawaii, but at the time of the attack American defenses were still far from adequate. In April and May 1941, one quarter of the Pacific Fleet was transferred to the Atlantic to help meet the threat to Lend-Lease shipping posed by German submarines. Between April and December of 1941, the U.S. gave thousands of patrol planes and anti-aircraft guns to allies, even though U.S. commanders in Hawaii were begging for them.

The Army was in charge of Oahu's defenses, but its air

Adm. Husband E. Kimmel, commander-in-chief of the U.S. Pacific Fleet from Feb. 1 to Dec. 17, 1941. He was censured by the Navy as an outgrowth of the Pearl Harbor attack and relieved of command. He applied for retirement and took no further part in the war. He died in 1968. USN

Lt. Gen. Walter C. Short, commanding general of the Army's Hawaiian Department at the time of the attack. Relieved of command on Dec. 17, 1941, he was never brought to trial to face allegations that he did not properly prepare for the possibility of a surprise attack.

force was woefully inadequate. Only six B-17 bombers were in flyable condition; 180 were considered necessary. Many Army fighters were obsolete. The Army had 82 three-inch anti-aircraft guns and needed 98; it had 20 37-millimeter guns and needed 135.

Lt. Gen. Walter Short, commander of the U.S. Army in Hawaii, had been advised of possible sabotage of his planes so he ordered them to be grouped together at Hickam and Wheeler. They would be much easier to guard than if they were scattered around the airfields.

Forty-five thousand men operated Oahu's coastal defense batteries, anti-aircraft guns, radar installations, air bases and other installations.

Five mobile stations employing newly invented radar equipment were in use by December 7, but they were inadequately staffed and the men were not yet fully trained. Gen. Walter Short, commander of the Hawaiian Department, had tried successfully to get permanent stations installed.

Navy aircraft patrolled the seas within a 600-mile radius of Oahu, but on the morning of the attack only three* PBY

*There were a total of seven PBYs in the air pre-attack. Three were on patrol of inshore/restricted areas and four were on maneuvers with the U.S. submarine *Gudgeon* near Lanai Island.

flying boats were on patrol, and none was north of the island where the Japanese fleet was launching aircraft. The Navy had only 49 patrol planes in flying condition and was further hampered by a shortage of crews and spare parts.

But if American forces were ill-equipped and undermanned, their main deficiency was that they just were not in a proper state of readiness to meet an attack with the resources they had. Partly because the Army and Navy were not under a unified command, coordination and cooperation were minimal. And—despite "war warnings" from Washington issued to the Pacific Fleet as early as November 27—there is evidence that U.S. officials did not give the Hawaii commanders all the available intelligence about a Japanese attack planned for sometime in December, possibly in Hawaii. For example, Joseph Grew, the American ambassador in Tokyo, had been advised by the Peruvian ambassador to Japan of a possible Japanese attack on Hawaii. Grew, however, apparently dismissed the information as another rumor; in any event, he thought he could keep hostilities from breaking out by keeping his ties with the moderates in the Japanese government.

He was, of course, dead wrong.

The *West Virginia* rounding Hospital Point as she
entered the Pearl Harbor naval base on 25 May 1935.
The huge 760-foot radio towers, a prominent feature of
the base for many years, were dismantled in 1937.
USN NH 77062

This peacetime panorama of Pearl Harbor on 30 Oct. 1941, looking east toward Honolulu, is just six weeks before the attack. Ford Island, East Loch Anchorage and Battleship Row are at left. The navy yard, sub base, supply depot and tank farms are to the left of the huge Hickam Field complex (right center) and the section base. Fort Kamehameha and the Pacific Ocean are extreme right. Note the two destroyers in the main channel passing through the anti-torpedo nets that guarded the harbor entrance. NA 80-G-182873

The Submarine Base and fuel oil storage tanks on Oct. 13, 1941. These would have been among the prime targets had the Japanese launched a third strike. The ever-cautious Admiral Nagumo, however, felt that his forces had accomplished their main mission, the destruction of the U.S. Battle Fleet. Leaving all naval support facilities undamaged would prove, in time, to be a fatal mistake by the Japanese. USN

Looking from the end of Drydock One in 1933, several ships are moored along the site of the soon-to-be constructed Ten-Ten Pier. It was so named because Drydock One was 1,010 feet long. USN

The administration building at the Naval Base, Pearl Harbor. USN

Floating Drydock YFD #2 in place on Oct. 30, 1940. The *Shaw* was in drydock here on Dec. 7. It took 45 days to tow the drydock from New Orleans to Pearl Harbor, a voyage of over 5,000 miles. USN

In Oct. 1940, Adm. James Richardson, right, visited Washington to protest the continued basing of the U.S. Fleet at Pearl Harbor. With him, from left, are Adm. Harry E. Yarnell, Ret. Adm. H. R. Stark and Secretary of the Navy Frank Knox. USN

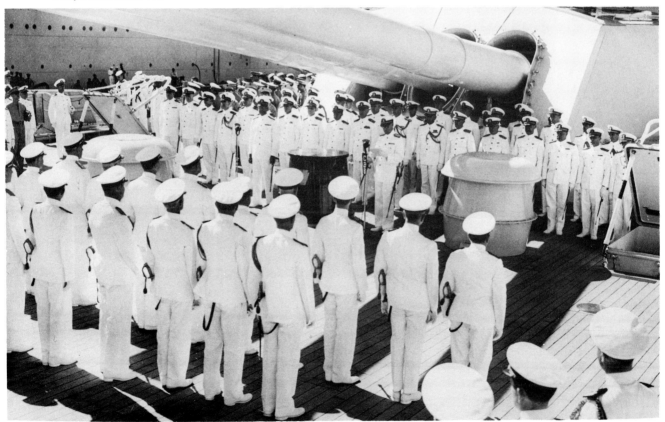

On Feb. 1, 1941, Adm. James O. Richardson turned over command of the Pacific Fleet to Adm. Husband E. Kimmel. The ceremony took place on the fleet flagship, the *Pennsylvania* at Pearl Harbor. HA

Gov. Joseph B. Poindexter, Hawaii's territorial governor from 1934 to 1942. At 3:30 p.m. on Dec. 7, he declared martial law in Hawaii at the urging of the Army commander. HA

I was present at Luke Field during the winter of 1931–32 when the Army and Navy conducted joint maneuvers during which the planes from the two carriers then in Navy inventory made a sneak attack on Pearl Harbor. The umpires ruled that all facilities were put out of commission. Our planes were not at the field and they searched and were credited with sinking one carrier. Several years ago I read an article written by a Japanese naval officer who was a Naval attaché and observer of the maneuvers and later a staff officer of the commander of the Japanese carrier force that attacked Pearl. He stated that the idea and pattern of the attack was largely initiated from his observations during the maneuvers.

—MAJ. KENNETH HORNER, AUS RET.
Phoenix, Oregon

URGENT -:- WARNING -:- URGENT

"BLACKOUT ENEMY" Planes will Simulate Attack on Your Island, Thursday Night, May 23rd, 1940, sometime between 8:30 and 9:00 p.m. When warning bells are rung or sirens are sounded, IMMEDIATELY put out all lights, inside and outside. TURN OFF ALL SIGNS. Don't use flashlights, matches, etc.

BLACKOUT COMPLETELY.

While this raid is only make-believe, do your part in this rehearsal
for an event we hope will never come.

"OUTBLACK THE LAST BLACKOUT"

NAINGET ·:· PAKAUNA ·:· NAINGET

"PANAGSIPNGET KABUSOR" NGA AIROPLANOS KASDALA RAOTEN DAYTA ISLA NGA YANMO INTON RABII TI JUEVES, MAYO 23, MANIPOD ORAS TI LAS 8:30 INGANAT LAS 9:00 P.M. INTON MANGNGEGYO DAGITI CAMPANAS NGA AGAWENG KEN PANAGTIMEK DAGITI SILBATOS, IDDEPENYO A DAGOS DAGITI SILAWYO ITI UNEG KEN RWAR. IDDEPENYO AMIN DAGITI MARKA NGA NASILAWAN. SAANKAY NGA AGGAMIT ITI LENTE, GURABIS, KEN DADDUMA PAY NGA UMAPOY. PAGBALINENYO NGA NASIPNGET.

(No man pay daytoy nga irarsot saan nga napaypayso, aramidenyo ti rebbengenyo iti daytoy a panagpadas tapno masagsaganakayo iti aniaman a dumteng, sapay koma ta saan met la a mapasamak.)

"NASIPSIPNGET PAY KOMA NGEM ITI DAYDI NAUDI A PANAGSIPNGET"

TERRITORIAL BLACKOUT COMMITTEES:

Ben F. Rush, General Chairman, Honolulu County;   H. C. Walters, General Chairman, Hawaii County;
Robt. E. Hughes, General Chairman, Maui County;   William Ellis, General Chairman, Kauai County.

A flyer announcing a blackout drill in Hawaii. Although the military was caught by surprise on Dec. 7, defense preparations had been going on for more than a year.
MILITARY SHOP OF HAWAII

Japanese Plans

The Watchword Was Secrecy

Emperor Hirohito, the supreme ruler of Japan, reviews troops in 1940. The new modern Japan had very close ties with its past. The Emperor was still revered as a god. USN

The Pearl Harbor attack was not an isolated incident, but part of an overall plan for the conquest of Southeast Asia and the promotion of what the Japanese called the Greater East Asia Co-Prosperity Sphere.

To have a free hand in establishing their control over the Dutch East Indies, Malaya, Thailand, the Philippines, Singapore, Hong Kong and the islands of the southern and western Pacific, the Japanese would have to neutralize the United States Pacific Fleet.

As early as 1940, Adm. Isoroku Yamamoto had given some thought to an attack on Pearl Harbor and had requested that Rear Adm. Takajiro Onishi, a naval aviator, investigate the possibilities.

Yamamoto knew America, having served a tour of duty in Washington, and was highly regarded by American officers. He had been vice-minister of the Japanese Navy before being named commander-in-chief of the Combined Fleet in 1941. A firm believer in the value of naval aircraft in modern warfare, he became convinced that a surprise aerial attack on Pearl Harbor was the best way to keep

the American fleet from interfering with Japanese plans in Southeast Asia.

The Japanese had been impressed with the success of the 24-plane British raid in which three Italian battleships were sunk at Taranto, with the loss of only two aircraft, in 1940. Such a raid by a large carrier strike force on a bottled-up U.S. fleet at Pearl Harbor seemed to promise similar results.

Some Japanese military planners wanted to concentrate all their naval strength to Southeast Asia instead of taking a chance at Hawaii, but Yamamoto's plan won out.

Onishi consulted Minoru Genda, an experienced carrier pilot and a brilliant aerial warfare tactician, who—after studying a working plan—concluded that a successful attack would be difficult but not impossible.

Yamamoto code-named the plan Operation "Z," after Admiral Togo's famous "Z" signal made on the eve of the Battle of Tsushima during the Russo-Japanese War. He selected Vice-Adm. Chuichi Nagumo to command the strike force.

Because Pearl Harbor was so shallow (45 feet), the Japanese had to devise torpedoes that would not nose into the bottom upon release from aircraft. Pilots and ordnance experts spent months on the problem. Finally, Cmdr. Mitsuo Fuchida, who was to lead the air attack, came up with an idea to place wooden fins on the torpedoes to guide them in shallow water.

Once the plan had been tentatively approved and worked out successfully on the war-game board, the best carrier pilots of the Navy were brought together for training. They were not told what the target was.

Absolute secrecy was required, for political as well as military reasons. Conceivably, the differences between the two countries might be settled only hours before the scheduled attack, thereby canceling it. If, on the other hand, there was to be war, the Japanese wanted their first blow to be a devastating surprise.

The operation was approved by Tokyo in September, and the following month the merchant ship *Taiyo Maru* sailed across the Pacific on the anticipated strike force route to make navigational observations and gather intelligence. It was happy to report that it sighted no other shipping during its mission.

For quite a while before the attack, the Japanese consulate in Honolulu had been supplying Tokyo with up-to-date intelligence about the military on Oahu.

As the fleet was secretly assembling in the remote Tankan Bay of the Kurile Islands, the Japanese made a point of showing that business between the U.S. and Japan was proceeding as usual. As late as December 2, when the attack force was well on its way, a merchant ship, the *Tatsuta Maru*, was dispatched for San Francisco as evidence of the con-

Adm. Isoroku Yamamoto, from an official portrait in 1943. He was the architect of the Pearl Harbor attack and commander-in-chief of the Japanese Combined Fleet. He was shot down and killed in the Solomons in April 1943 by American planes. USN

tinuing friendly relations between the two countries. But she had secret orders to turn around and sail back to Japan on the night of December 7.

A powerful task force was assembled to ensure that the attack was successful. Six carriers—*Akagi, Kaga, Soryu, Zuikaku, Hiryu* and *Shokaku*—carried 441 war planes. The screening unit comprised a light cruiser and nine destroyers. Two battleships and two heavy cruisers constituted the support force, and three I-class submarines the patrol unit. Eight tankers accompanied the force to the point of refueling. An additional 27 submarines, plus five midget submarines of the Special Submarine Attack Unit, carried orders to support the main body and to inflict damage on American warships. The task force was the mightiest fleet ever assembled in the Pacific.

A northerly course was selected, away from the normal shipping lanes. The force planned to sail within 200 miles of Oahu's northern coast and launch its planes on December 7. To hit the American fleet early on Sunday morning—a time thought to be the best for a surprise attack—the fleet would have to be at its launching point before first light.

It was a gamble, sailing so close to American fighter and bomber bases, which would surely have aircraft patrolling the seas. But the risk was considered necessary, given the

Vice-Adm. Chuichi Nagumo, commander-in-chief of the Japanese First Carrier Strike Force, which carried out the Pearl Harbor attack. Instead of sending in the third attack wave, he decided to retire to Japan. He committed suicide on Saipan in July 1944. USN

The Japanese exchange ship *Tatsuta Maru*, flagship of the NYK line, was used as a deceptive maneuver. It left Japan on Dec. 2, supposedly bound for San Francisco with American evacuees from the Orient. They were to be exchanged for Japanese nationals in the United States. The captain, however had orders to return to Japan Dec. 7, and to observe radio silence en route. This is a post-Pearl Harbor attack photo. NA

short range and limited fuel capacity of the carrier planes.

On November 26 the strike force began its long journey from Etorofu Island. Tankers refueled destroyers every day until the last pre-attack fueling on December 6, then went to a rendezvous point to again refuel every day from December 8. Other ships had carried drums of fuel to feed their hungry boilers for the long round trip. No longer slowed down by the fuel-heavy tankers, the fleet picked up another 5 knots speed to make the launching point on time.

On December 2 at 5:30 p.m., Admiral Nagumo had received the signal "Climb Mount Niitaka," which meant that all the diplomatic efforts had failed and he was to proceed with the attack.

On December 7—it was already December 8 in Japan—float planes launched from the cruisers at 5:30 a.m. flew over Pearl Harbor and Lahaina roads to make sure the fleet was indeed at Pearl.

At 6:15 a.m. the first carrier aircraft were launched on their flight into history.

Japanese Monograph #97

If the destruction of enemy land-based air strength progresses favorably, repeated attacks will be made immediately and thus decisive results will be achieved.

In the event a powerful enemy surface fleet appears, it will be attacked.

2. *Organization of the Air Attack Units.*

(See Chart 2)

3. *Targets*

a. *The First Wave Units*

The targets for the hi-level and torpedo Kates will be battleships and aircraft carriers; the order of targets will be battleships and then aircraft carriers.

The dive bombers will attack the enemy land-based air strength according to the following assignments:

The Shokaku Vals: Hangars and aircraft on Ford Island.

The 16 Zuikaku Vals: Hangars and aircraft on Wheeler Field.

The targets of Fighter Units will be enemy aircraft in the air and on the ground.

b. *The Second Wave Units*

The hi-level Kates will attack the enemy air bases according to the following assignments:

The Shokaku Kates: Aircraft and hangars on Kaneohe and Ford Island.

The Zuikaku Kates: Hangars and aircraft on Hickam Field.

The targets for the dive bombers will be limited to enemy aircraft carriers. If the number of targets is insufficient, they will select targets in the order of cruisers and battleship.

The Fighter Units will attack the enemy aircraft in the air and on the ground.

4. *Attack Procedure*

a. *The First Wave Units*

(1) With the element of surprise as the principle, attacks will be carried out by the torpedo unit and bomber units and then the dive bombers.

(2) During the initial phase of the attack, the Fighter Units, in one formation, storm the enemy skies about the same time as the Kate units, and contact and destroy chiefly the enemy interceptor planes.

In the event that no enemy aircraft are encountered in the air, the units will immediately shift to the strafing of parked aircraft as follows:

Akagi and Kaga Fighter Units: Hickam Field and Barbers Point (Ewa).

Soryu and Hiryu Fighter Units: Wheeler Field and Barbers Point (Ewa).

Shokaku and Zuikaku Fighter Units: Kaneohe

Total Participants
BY DAVID AIKEN

FIRST WAVE

High-level Kates: 49 participants (fifty assigned, one mechanical abort):
  Akagi: 15—Three Buntai of five aircraft each. Cmdr. Mitsuo Fuchida
  Kaga: 14—Three Buntai of five aircraft each, one mechanical abort. Lt. Cmdr. Takashi Hashiguchi
  Soryu: 10—Two Buntai of five aircraft each. Lt. Heijiro Abe
  Hiryu: 10—Two Buntai of five aircraft each. Lt. Cmdr. Tadashi Kusumi

Torpedo carrying Kates: 40 participants (no aborts):
  Akagi: 12—Two Buntai of 6 each. Lt. Cmdr. Shigeharu Murata
  Kaga: 12—Two Buntai of 6 each. Lt. Kazuyoshi Kitajima
  Soryu: eight—Two Buntai of four each. Lt. Tsuyoshi Nagai
  Hiryu: eight—Two Buntai of four each. Lt. Hirata Matsumura

Dive bomber Vals: 51 participants (54 assigned, three mechanical aborts):
  Shokaku: 26—Three Buntai of nine each, one mechanical abort. Lt. Cmdr. Kakuichi Takahashi
  Zuikaku: 25—Three Buntai (27 aircraft), two mechanical aborts. Lt. Akira Sakamoto

Fighters Zero/Zeke: 43 participants (45 assigned, two mechanical aborts, 12 retained for combat air patrol):
  Akagi: nine—One Buntai of nine. Lt. Cmdr. Shigeru Itaya
  Kaga: nine—One Buntai of nine. Lt. Yoshio Shiga
  Soryu: eight—One Buntai of nine, one mechanical abort. Lt. Masaji Suganami
  Hiryu: six—Two Shotai of three each, three retained for combat air patrol. Lt. Kiyokuma Okajima
  Shokaku: five—Two Shotai of three each, one mechanical abort, three retained for combat air patrol. Lt. Tadashi Kaneko
  Zuikaku: six—Three Shotai of two each, three retained for combat air patrol. Lt. Masao Sato

SECOND WAVE

High-level Kates: 54 participants (no aborts).
  Shokaku: 27—Three Buntai of nine each. Lt. Tatsuo Ichihara
  Zuikaku: 27—Three Buntai of nine each. Lt. Cmdr. Shigekazu Shimazaki

Dive bomber/Vals: 78 participants (81 assigned, one mechanical abort and two aborts after launch):
  Agaki: 18—Two Buntai of nine each. Lt. Takehiko Chihaya
  Kaga: 26—Three Buntai of nine each, one mechanical abort. Lt. Saburo Makino
  Soryu: 17—Two Buntai of nine each, one abort after launch. Lt. Cmdr. Takashige Egusa
  Hiryu: 17—Two Buntai of nine each, one abort after launch. Lt. Shun Nakagawa

Fighters Zero/Zeke: 35 participants (36 assigned, one abort after launch).
  Akagi: nine—One Buntai of nine. Lt. Saburo Shindo
  Kaga: nine—One Buntai of nine. Lt. Yasushi Nikaido
  Soryu: nine—One Buntai of nine. Lt. Fusata Iida
  Hiryu: eight—One Buntai of nine, one abort after launch. Lt. Sumio Nono

Totals

Japanese Aircraft:
  441 Aircraft aboard carriers (three spare aircraft per type).
  389 Carrier aircraft used in operations.
  360 assigned to attack.
  Seven known mechanical aborts.
  353 deck spotted.
  Three aborts on launch (second wave).
  350 in attack.
  Plus two cruiser seaplanes (advance reconn).
  352 above Oahu.
  Plus four cruiser and battleship seaplanes (reconn between Niihau and task force).
  39 Combat air patrol.
  395 above Hawaiian waters.

Aircraft on the carriers:	Kate	Val	Zero	Total
Akagi	27+3*	18+3	18+3	72
Kaga	27+3	27+3	18+3	81
Soryu	18+3	18+3	18+3	63
Hiryu	18+3	18+3	18+3	63
Shokaku	27+3	27+3	18+3	81
Zuikaku	27+3	27+3	18+3	81
TOTAL	144+18	135+18	108+18	
	162	153	126	441

*Three spare aircraft per type

Utilized:

include CAP	Kate		Val	Zero		+CAP
Akagi	15+12=27		18	9+9=18		+3:21
Kaga	14+12=26		26	9+9=18		+3:21
Soryu	10+8 =18		17	8+9=17		+3:21
Hiryu	10+8 =18		17	6+8=14		+6:21
Shokaku	27	27	26	5	5	+12:18
Zuikaku	27	27	25	6	6	+12:18
		143	129	43+35=78		+39

TOTAL 350 attack vets
39 CAP
389 utilized

Japanese Ships Assigned to "Hawaii Operation"

Type	Name	Date and Place Sunk by U.S. Navy
CARRIERS	*Akagi*	June 5, 1942, Battle of Midway
	Kaga	June 4, 1942, Battle of Midway
	Soryu	June 4, 1942, Battle of Midway
	Hiryu	June 5, 1942, Battle of Midway
	Shokaku	June 19, 1944, Philippine Sea
	Zuikaku	Oct. 25, 1944, Leyte Gulf
BATTLESHIPS	*Hiei*	Nov. 13, 1942, Guadalcanal
	Kirishima	Nov. 15, 1942, Guadalcanal
MIDGET SUBS	*I-16A*	Dec. 7, 1941, Pearl Harbor
	I-18A	Dec. 7, 1941, Pearl Harbor
	I-20A	Dec. 7, 1941, Pearl Harbor
	I-22A	Dec. 7, 1941, Pearl Harbor
	I-24A	Dec. 8, 1941, Pearl Harbor
DESTROYERS	*Isokaze*	Apr. 7, 1945, East China Sea
	Tanikaze	June 9, 1944, Tawi Tawi
	Hamakaze	Apr. 7, 1945, East China Sea
	Kasumi	Apr. 7, 1945, East China Sea
	Arare	July 5, 1942, Aleutian Islands
	Kagero	May 8, 1943, Solomon Islands
	Shiranuhi	Oct. 27, 1944, Luzon Area P.I.
	Akigumo	Apr. 11, 1944, Celebes Sea
	Urakaze	Nov. 21, 1944, Formosa
	Akebono	Nov. 13, 1944, Palau area
	Ushio	Surrendered at Yokosuka
	Sazanami	Jan. 14, 1944, Yap
TANKERS	*Kyokuto Maru*	Survived to surrender
	Kenyo Maru	Jan. 14, 1944, Palau area
	Kokuyo Maru	July 30, 1944, Sulu Sea
	ShinkokuMaru	Feb. 17, 1944, Caroline Islands
	Akebono Maru	Mar. 30, 1944, Palau Area
	Toho Maru	June 15, 1945, Gulf of Siam
	Nihon Maru	Jan. 14, 1944, Bismarks
	Toei Maru	Jan. 18, 1943, Rabaul area

NOTES: The three spare Zeros on each carrier were available for CAP and thus assigned by *Akagi, Kaga, Soryu,* and *Hiryu.*

The 5th CV Division also had those available, but only assigned 12 each while keeping the spares in reserve. Mechanical aborts also lowered the total participants and may be a portion of the "reserve" spare total.

Returning Zeros from Oahu action were rapidly rearmed and fueled, thus augmented the CAP force. Even three VAL dive bombers aided the CAP effort!

	Name	Date and Place
SUBMARINES	*I-1*	Jan. 29, 1943, Guadalcanal
	I-2	Apr. 7, 1944, New Ireland
	I-3	Dec. 9, 1942, Guadalcanal
	I-4	Dec. 20, 1942, New Britain
	I-5	July 19, 1944, Guam
	I-6	July 14, 1944, Marianas I.
	I-7	July 5, 1943, Aleutian I.
	I-8	Mar. 31, 1945, Okinawa
	I-9	June 11, 1943, Aleutian I.
	I-10	July 4, 1944, Saipan
	I-15	Nov. 2, 1942, Solomon I.
	I-16	May 19, 1944, Solomon I.
	I-17	Aug. 19, 1943, Noumea
	I-18	Feb. 11, 1943, Solomon I.
	I-19	Oct. 18, 1943, Gilbert I.
	I-20	Oct. 1, 1943, New Hebrides
	I-21	Nov. 29, 1943, Tarawa
	I-22	Oct. 1, 1942, Solomons
	I-23	Feb. 26, 1942 – operational loss
	I-24	June 7, 1943, Aleutians
	I-25	Sept. 3, 1943, New Hebrides
	I-26	Oct. 27, 1944, Leyte
	I-68	July 27, 1943, Bismarks
	I-69	April 4, 1944, Truk
	I-70	Dec. 10, 1941, N.E. Oahu
	I-71	Feb. 1, 1944, Solomons
	I-72	Nov. 11, 1942, Guadalcanal
	I-73	Jan. 27, 1942, Midway
	I-74	April 3, 1944, Truk
	I-75	Feb. 5, 1944, Marshals
CRUISERS	*Tone*	July 24, 1945, Kure
	Chikuma	Oct. 25, 1944, Leyte Gulf
	Katori	Feb. 17, 1944, Truk
	Abukuma	Oct. 26, 1944, Surigao Straight

United States involvement in World War II was only hours away when Homer L. Kisner (right), Rochefort's radio intelligence traffic chief, warned that Japan's navy was nearly on a "war time basis." Kisner prepared his last peacetime chronology from radio intercepts gathered by his trained force of 64 radio operators. At 0755 the morning of Dec. 7, the Japanese naval task force which had been under radio surveillance by Rochefort for nearly a month, struck Pearl Harbor.
COURTESY ROBERT STINNETT

Station H
6 Dec. 1941.

CHRONOLOGY, Cont'd.

Fourth Fleet : It has been definitely established by traffic study that CinC 4th Fleet is in the Truk area. Several times traffic routing indicated that part of the Staff of CinC 4th Fleet was at Jaluit. It is possible that this command has been split-up for better administration of all operations in the South Seas. The Kamoi (with Commanding Officer, Chitose Air Corps aboard) is in the Jaluit area.

Traffic continues to be exchanged between several 4th Fleet units and Commands in the Indo-China area.

Fifth Fleet : Ominato has been heard working the flagship and at least one other unit of the 5th Fleet for the last few days. This fleet has been based at Chichijima for some time. It is probable that part of this force has remained at Chichijima; it is known that XS06 (Airron attached to 5th Fleet) is there.

General : At 0430, Tokyo was heard using 32Kcs, dual with 12330 Kcs, for UTU broadcast of traffic. This broadcast was discontinued at 1800, but 7285 Kcs (M) was immediately brought up and used until 1900, when it was secured. This broadcast was used in addition to Tokyo's regular UTU. Tokyo also broadcasted traffic on 6665 Kcs (A) during the evening.

Saipan, Takao and Ominato were also heard broadcasting traffic to units in their vicinities. The use of this method of delivering messages tends to keep unknown the positions of vessels afloat, and is probably one of the first steps toward placing the operations of the Navy on a war-time basis.

SECRET

-17-

A SPY FINDS EASY PICKINGS

In July 1941, while serving as a lieutenant commander with the staff of the Third Imperial Fleet, then blockading mainland China, I received orders assigning me to the personnel section of the ministry of the navy. This was bad news; it meant a desk job.

Two months later, in September, the office of naval operations issued me my real orders: I was to travel to Hawaii and report on Pearl Harbor. Our navy already had extensive knowledge of the American installations there, but the information at its disposal had been gathered by civilians unversed in naval matters. My task was to supplement this information with technical details. Without specifically saying so, my orders made me a spy.

The boat on which I was to travel, the **Taiyo Maru,** was sailing from Yokohama to repatriate Japanese citizens from Hawaii. There were several hundred American families on board, going home because of the precarious political situation.

Officially I had become the new purser of the **Taiyo Maru** and I soon found that I was not the only secret agent on board: Commander Maejima, a specialist in submarine warfare, was traveling as ship's doctor. Besides the top executives of the shipping company, only the captain and two or three of his aides had been told of our real assignment. Maejima spent most of his time reading medical books; he was worried lest some passenger in need of medical help should call on him. I had no such problem since my job as a purser required no special knowledge.

We weighed anchor on Oct. 20. The course we took was most unusual, for we had been ordered to sail straight north and turn eastward in the vicinity of Etorofu island, one of the Kuriles. (Today we know that the **Taiyo Maru** was charting the route for the Japanese task force which was to attack Pearl Harbor. During the voyage the ship's doctor and purser were busy studying the winds and the atmospheric pressure, recording the pitch and the roll of the ship, and trying to find suitable areas in which to refuel a task force, a complex operation in those days).

At 165 degrees longitude west, the **Taiyo Maru** veered southward, maintaining a speed of 14 knots. Soon the seas became calmer. From then on I concentrated on a new phase of my work--trying to locate the likeliest spots for dispatching carrier-based planes. On the entire journey from Japan to Hawaii we did not encounter a single vessel--which constituted the most important information I obtained during the voyage, for we had expected to meet a number of American and Soviet transports.

The **Taiyo Maru** was directed by the Honolulu harbor command to tie up at the pier nearest Pearl Harbor. I hurried to the bridge, and there was Pearl Harbor right before my eyes. I could see everything. Luckily, the **Taiyo Maru** was commissioned at the time when superstructures were built high above the water line; from my vantage point on the bridge I could spot every ship entering and leaving or landing at Rogers and Hickam fields. I didn't even need binoculars. 'I turned to "Doc" Maejima: "It's too good to be true. There must be a catch. Watch out."

Later that day we received indications that caution was indeed warranted: Members of the crew on shore leave reported they had been shadowed by policemen in uniform and followed by plainclothesmen on motorcycles. Maejima and I agreed that it would be too risky for us to leave the ship and attempt to gather information in Honolulu and Pearl Harbor.

On board we took extreme precautions. We posted an officer on deck and put a direct telephone line from his observation point to the captain's cabin. As soon as any suspicious person approached the ship, the officer on duty would alert us. Maejima and I discussed our observations and exchanged information only in the captain's cabin. An alert from the sentinel on deck immediately stopped all conversation. We also carefully tested our telephone lines and made sure they were not tapped.

When these precautions had been taken we invited Consul General Kita to visit us on board. We explained our assignment to him and asked for his cooperation; he at once agreed. There was no difficulty about maintaining communications between the ship and the consulate; since the **Taiyo Maru** was a reparation vessel for Japanese nationals in Hawaii, it was natural for the consul general's staff to come on board every day. And each day one staff member would act as a special courier through whom the consul general supplied us with information. We received this information in the captain's cabin and attempted to check every item that concerned the Pearl Harbor installations by going up to the bridge and looking things over with our own eyes.

On the second morning the local newspapers gave us a rude shock. According to a front page story, a Japanese submarine had been observed operating in Pearl Harbor waters. There were other unconfirmed reports claiming that Japanese naval officers in various disguises had been seen loitering in some areas on the West Coast of the United States.

Even greater caution seemed to be called for; in the circumstances United States security officers might raid the ship at any moment. We therefore decided not to keep written records, relying exclusively on memory for both our own observations and the written reports transmitted by consular officials. We committed every line of these reports to memory before destroying this evidence of our activities . . .

On Nov. 3, just 24 hours after the alleged sighting of the Japanese submarine had appeared in the local press, it was denied by the United States Navy. Maejima and I sighed with relief . . .

Looking back, I think that in those days, the United States was easy prey for us. For example, on Nov. 3, I received an aerial photograph of Pearl Harbor that had been taken from a tourist plane stationed at John Rogers field. The picture was said to have been taken on Oct. 21, 1941, 10 days before our arrival. All this made me uneasy. Why did we receive such valuable information? I felt as if we might be walking into a gigantic trap.

From my vantage point on the bridge, I studied Pearl Harbor. I saw eight battleships, three carriers, eleven cruisers, and miscellaneous auxiliary craft, anchored at the harbor or moored to the piers. I had checked our own information, according to which 500 United States planes were based on Oahu and 114 flying boats at Kaneohe; from visual observation I was able to verify that 150 bombers were stationed at Hickam, 200 fighters at Wheeler, and 30 trainers at Bellows. Lastly, I studied the hangars and other installations. During my walks on deck I was also memorizing the schedule and the routines of the American air patrols. The hard work involved in checking, counter-checking, and double-checking every bit of information and every figure received from agents in our espionage network paid off: The data I finally pieced together turned out to be extremely accurate.

We had been scheduled to sail from Honolulu on Saturday afternoon, Nov. 4, but I wanted to see the harbor on a Sunday morning. The captain agreed to delay our departure and slowed down loading operations to justify the delay. This aroused no suspicion among the Americans. After all, it was only a delay in the sailing of a merchantman.

On Sunday I was up early. The master plan for the Pearl Harbor attack called for action on a Sunday, on the assumption that the holiday routine would relax the vigilance of the American forces. My job was to verify this assumption. And on that Sunday morning Pearl Harbor was indeed relaxed. The decks of the ships at anchor were deserted and the only movement I could detect was the fluttering of the flags. Our hunch had proved correct.

We sailed that evening, but even at sea I took no chances. Only the most important information had been put on paper. This paper was rolled into strings which lay near the ash tray in my cabin so that I could burn them at a moment's notice. My action was based on a recent incident off Tokyo Bay when a Japanese merchant vessel had been boarded by British sailors searching for German nationals. It could happen to us.

On the homeward voyage the **Taiyo Maru** continued its charting job. Our route took us slightly south of the course we had taken on our way to Hawaii, and this was the route that was used by the Nagumo task force after the attack on Pearl Harbor.

After an uneventful trip we arrived in Yokohama on Nov. 17. I immediately reported to headquarters and was ordered forthwith to the battleship **Hiei**. Two days later the **Hiei** sailed from Kisarazu, situated at the opposite end of Tokyo Bay from Yokohama. She was to join the task force, which was then assembling in the Hitokappu (Tankan) Bay off Etorofu Island.

It was in Hitokappu Bay aboard the carrier **Akagi,** flagship of the task force, that the final strategy conference before Pearl Harbor was held on Nov. 23. First I reported on my "reconnaissance" of Pearl Harbor. Then I briefed our pilots, illustrating my instructions with a relief map of the city and harbor. I also gave them details on roofing materials used on the hangars--details I had obtained from some of the Japanese passengers on the **Taiyo Maru** who had worked on their construction.

On Nov. 25 Adm. Isoroku Yamamoto, commander-in-chief of the Imperial Fleet, ordered the task force to sail next day.

I spent that night aboard the **Akagi** At 2 a.m. on Nov. 26 I was awakened by an orderly who told me that Vice-Adm. Chuichi Nagumo wanted to see me immediately.

Admiral Nagumo looked grim. After apologizing for rousing me at such an hour, he said: "I want to be absolutely certain of one thing. Are you sure the American fleet is still in Pearl Harbor? Can you be sure that the fleet is anchored in the harbor and is not moving to an anchorage outside?"

"I feel absolutely certain, sir, that the American fleet is in Pearl Harbor. All the information I obtained supports my conviction on this point."

Later that morning the Nagumo force left the icy waters of Hitokappu Bay. I had transferred from the **Akagi** to the gunboat **Kunashiri** and was returning home. The gunboat's crew kept asking me whether "the big maneuvers were now over." I replied in the affirmative. Pearl Harbor was still a tightly kept secret in Japan.

Suguru Suzuki
former Commander of the Japanese Navy

The machine that came to be known as "Purple" broke the Japanese diplomatic code in 1941. There were only six Purple machines made in 1941. One went to London, two were in the hands of Navy Intelligence, the War Department's Signal Intelligence Service had two and the sixth went to the Philippines. The Commanders, Admiral Kimmel and General Short, did not have direct access to "Magic" intelligence. If they had, they would have had their forces in a better state of preparedness to meet the Japanese onslaught. This photo is of the actual Japanese machine recovered from the Japanese embassy in Berlin in May 1945. The American "purple" machine is still classified. NA

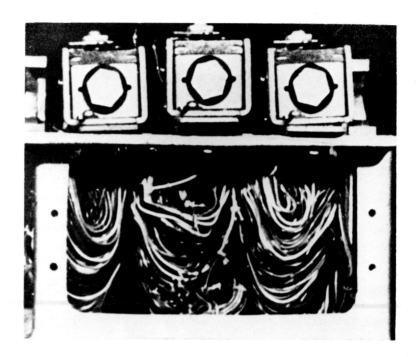

The Four Winds Code Executes

A modest-sized Netherlands East Indies Army Code Service, headed by a Captain Verkuyl, operated in early 1941 in an underground communications center at the Higher Technical College situated on Dago road in the city of Bandung, Java, N.E.I. The captain and his wife, Nancy, had lived in Japan for almost eight years and they were both fluent in the Japanese language. They had also studied Japanese cryptology and thus worked as a team for the N.E.I. code service. It was about six months before the war, in May 1941, when Nancy Verkuyl made an important discovery. She had learned how to proceed with the decipher of a major Japanese code. A Dutch-Indonesian lady had cracked codes! Because of the breakthrough found by Nancy Verkuyl the code service was enlarged as quickly as possible, but it took many more months of hard painstaking work by teams of cryptoanalysts to determine they had indeed broken an important and reliable Japanese code. By summer of 1941 the N.E.I. code service worked full shifts around the clock intercepting and decoding Japanese messages from all corners of the Far East. It was in early Oct. 1941 that through one of these intercepts it was learned that the Japanese had instructed their own units scattered throughout the Far East that from that moment on their units also had to monitor Radio Tokyo weather broadcasts. In these weather reports their would be a code-in-voice hidden, and these would only be transmitted in sudden emergencies. There would be little time left for action and therefore this code would be in-voice, in the form of wind sentences, in the middle as well as at the end of the weather report. They would mean to execute within 72 hours.

NORTH WIND CLOUDY
(Kita No Kaze Kumori) execute for: attack Russia.

WEST WIND CLEAR
(Nishi No Kaze Hare) execute for: attack British.

SOUTH WIND STORMY
(Minami No Kazi Arashi)
execute for: attack Dutch East Indies.

EAST WIND RAIN
(Higashi No Kaze Ame) execute for: attack Pearl Harbor.

Naturally, this ominous message caused considerable excitement and extra alertness at the N.E.I. code service. The tension grew.

It was on Dec. 5, 1941 (Java Time), that the message was received: Higashi No Kaze Ame (East Wind Rain) meaning that within 72 hours Pearl Harbor would be attacked. The chief military intelligence officer of the U.S. Army in Bandung was Col. E.R. Thorpe, and he states in his book *East Wind Rain* that he did send this crucial warning to Washington. He states: "I suppose the most important thing I ever did as an army intelligence officer was to notify Washington of the forthcoming attack on Pearl Harbor."

This war warning was received in Washington on Dec. 4, 1941 (it is one day earlier in Washington than in Java) as is testified to by Captain Safford, U.S. Navy and is also acknowledged by Gen. Albert Wedemeyer, U.S. Army, Chief of Army Operations.   KAREL N. RINK

Japanese Ambassador Nomura and Special Envoy Kurusu leave the White House, possibly on Nov. 26, 1941, after the proposals they hoped would avert war had been rejected. Unbeknownst to the two men, their mission would be a fruitless one on Dec. 7 when they met with Cordell Hull on the "Day of Infamy." USN

Kurusu & Nomura

Saburo Kurusu was sent by the Japanese government to help Ambassador Nomura negotiate with the United States government in November 1941. He had been the Japanese ambassador to Germany and had signed the Tripartite Partnership between Germany, Italy and Japan in 1940. He married an American, Alice Jay, in New York in 1914. She spent the war years in Japan, after the couple was repatriated there in 1942. Their son, Ryo, was in the Japanese Air Force, and after making a forced landing in Japan due to a mechanical failure on his airplane, was beaten to death by local peasants. Because of his looks, they thought he was an American. Kurusu died in 1954.

Kichisaburo Nomura was a Japanese Admiral and Ambassador to the United States during World War I and a delegate to the Versailles Peace Treaty Conference in 1917 and the 1922 Washington Naval Conference. He died in 1964.

This ad appearing in a Honolulu newspaper before the attack was attributed to a Japanese spy as a coded message. Notice how it has been decoded. This supposed message has been totally discounted.

Gen. Hideki Tojo

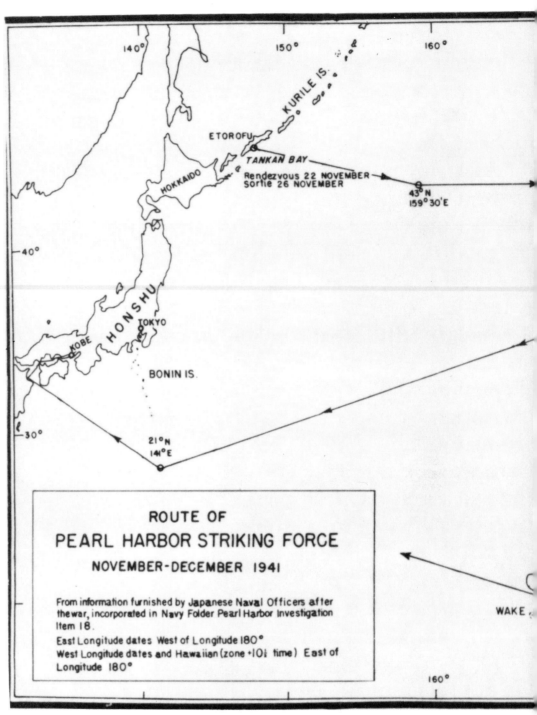

ROUTE OF
PEARL HARBOR STRIKING FORCE
NOVEMBER-DECEMBER 1941

From information furnished by Japanese Naval Officers after
the war, incorporated in Navy Folder Pearl Harbor Investigation
Item 18.
East Longitude dates West of Longitude 180°
West Longitude dates and Hawaiian (zone +10½ time) East of
Longitude 180°

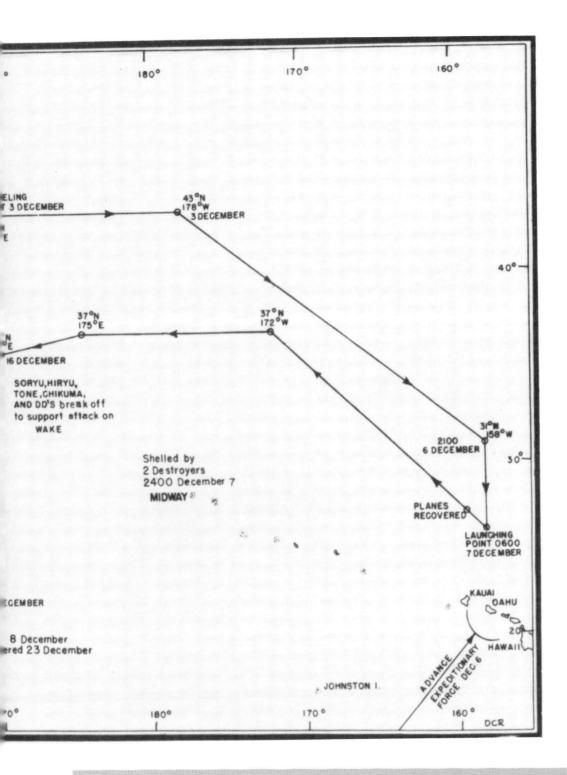

180° 170° 160°

EELING
T 3 DECEMBER

43°N
178°W
3 DECEMBER

40°

37°N
175°E

NE
E

37°N
172°W

16 DECEMBER

SORYU, HIRYU,
TONE, CHIKUMA,
AND DD'S break off
to support attack on
WAKE

31°N
158°W

2100
6 DECEMBER

30°

Shelled by
2 Destroyers
2400 December 7
MIDWAY

PLANES
RECOVERED

LAUNCHING
POINT 0600
7 DECEMBER

ECEMBER

KAUAI
OAHU

20

8 December
ered 23 December

HAWAII

ADVANCE
EXPEDITIONARY
FORCE DEC. 6

JOHNSTON I.

0° 180° 170° 160°

DCR

The Military Careers of Minoru Genda

From Naval Institute Proceedings, April 1990

Born in Kake, Hiroshima Prefecture on 16 August 1904, Minoru Genda entered the Naval Academy at Eta Jima in August, 1921, graduating three years later. He received his ensigns commission in Decem- ber 1925 after having served nine-month tours of duty in the first-class coast defense ship *Izumo* and the light cruiser *Oi*. Following one year in the battle- ship *Ise*, he reported to Yokosuka for successive assignments at the Naval Gunnery School and the Naval Torpedo and Mine School. In July, 1927 he rejoined the *Izumo* as assistant navigator.

Genda's career as a naval aviator began in December 1928 when, as a second lieutenant, he reported for primary flight training at Naval Air Station (NAS) Kasumigaura, transferring one year later to NAS Yokosuka for advanced training in fighters. He joined the fighter squadron on board the carrier *Akagi* in February 1930. Returning to NAS Yokosuka as a flight instructor late in 1931. First Lieutenant Genda organized and led "Genda's Circus" of navy aerial acrobats which performed throughout Japan. In April 1933 he began 18 months of duty on the light cruiser *Ryujo*, after which he went back to Yokosuka as squadron commander and flight instructor.

Now a lieutenant commander, Genda entered the Imperial Naval Staff College in late 1935 and quickly earned the nickname "madman Genda" for his outspoken views on the supremacy of aircraft over the battleship. Immediately upon his graduation in July 1937, the war in China broke out, whereupon he served briefly on the staff of the Second Air Force and at the headquarters of the Third Fleet. He reported as wing commander at Yokosuka in January 1938, transferring in April to the Torpedo School as instructor, his genius in torpedoes now well-established. Genda reported as assistant naval attaché for air at the Japanese embassy in London the following December. At the end of this tour, November 1940, he was impressed by the British carrier-based torpedo plane attack which crippled the Italian battleship fleet at Taranto.

Reporting as air operations officer to Commander, First Carrier Squadron, later that month and in the rank of commander, Genda began developing carrier tactics for the fleet while on board the flagship *Kaga*. Early in 1941 Rear Admiral Takijiro Onishi, chief of staff of the shore-based Eleventh Air Fleet, asked his advice about a proposal by Admiral Isoroku Yamamoto, Commander in Chief Combined Fleet, for a surprise carrier raid on Pearl Harbor to initiate war with the United States. Genda studied the idea for ten days before endorsing it. In April he became air operations officer of the new fast carrier striking force. First Air Fleet, and the next month initiated the study and testing of aerial torpedoes to make short, shallow runs in the 30- to 45-foot-deep Hawaiian anchorage. He was Admiral Nagumo's key adviser on the flagship *Akagi* during the attack. Genda's carrier tactics worked equally well in the conquest of Southeast Asia, including air strikes in Ceylon and Port Darwin, Australia. He drew up the air plan for the Midway operation but was confined to sick bay with pneumonia at the outset. On strike day, 4 June 1942, he nevertheless managed to climb to the flag bridge, where, beset with fever and clothed in pajamas, he was embraced by Admiral Nagumo who followed his advice. Later in the day, however, he was evacuated from the stricken *Akagi*.

The next month Genda became air group commander on the carrier *Zuikaku*, from which he participated in the Battle of the Eastern Solomons in August. In October he moved to Rabaul as air operations officer of Eleventh Air Fleet for two crucial months of the Guadalcanal-Solomons Campaign. He transferred in December to Tokyo for duty with the air operations section, Naval General Staff and Imperial Headquarters, coordinating air defenses in Southeast Asia and making trips to the East Indies, Philippines, and Indochina between May 1943 and the end of 1944.

In January 1945 Genda took command of the 343rd Fighter Group of the last veteran navy pilots and flying new Shiden-kai ("George") fighters charged with defending Tokyo. When U.S. carrier planes from Task Force 58 struck Tokyo and Kure in March, his planes inflicted unusually heavy casualties on the Grumman F6F-5 Hellcats in dogfights. But the war was lost, and by its end in August, Genda had achieved the rank of captain. He was transferred to the reserve in November 1945.

Called upon to testify before the U.S. Strategic Bombing Survey that autumn, Genda revealed many of the details of Japan's wartime operations. To charges of inconsistencies in his accounts, he explained in 1969 that he and his peers had been called to testify with practically no food to sustain them—only a small tin of rice for each witness. Virtually starving, he had difficulty concentrating on the questions. During the hearings, he was questioned, and befriended, by U.S. Navy Commander Thomas H. Moorer, who was Chief of Naval Operations 24 years later, and arranged for Genda to visit the United States.

After the formal Treaty of San Francisco, in July 1954, Genda was commissioned a major general in the Japanese Air Self-Defense Force as Deputy Chief of Staff for Material. At the end of the following year he assumed command of the First Fighter Wing and qualified in the F-86F Sabrejet used by his command. Promoted to lieutenant general, in July 1957 Genda became commander of Japan's Air Defense Command, and exactly two years later was made Chief of Staff of the Air Self-Defense Force in the rank of general. Although he retired from active duty in April 1962, by the time of his visit to the United States he had checked out in all major Western fighters except the F-4 Phantom II.

CLARK G. REYNOLDS

Ford Island

Holocaust at Hangar #6

In the opening minutes of the attack, one of the first bombs to fall hit Seaplane Hangar #6 on the southwest point of Ford Island. Planes parked on the ramp were set afire by other bomb hits from nine *Shokaku* VAL dive bombers. One bomb caused a hangar door to fall across a Dutch PBY destined for Java. Two other Dutch PBYs had already arrived at Midway and one was damaged in the shelling of the island. The survivor returned to Oahu on Monday to assist in Hawaii's defense. USN

*F*ord Island—at one time known as Mokuumeume (Island of Strife), Rabbit Island, Marin's Island and Little Goats Island—lies in the middle of Pearl Harbor's East Loch.

Although only a mile and a quarter long and half as wide, it has played an important part in the military history of the area.

Don F. Francisco de Paula y Maria, a Spaniard who purchased the island in 1791, was the first of several owners. James Dowset bought the island in 1865 and then sold it to Carolina Jackson by trust deed for $1. In 1886, Dr. Seth Porter Ford, for whom the island would eventually be named, married Miss Jackson and assumed ownership. It was sold to the Ii estate upon Ford's death and leased to the Oahu Sugar Company until the United States entered World War I in 1917.

At that time the U.S. Army took it over and established a west-side airfield named for Lt. Frank Luke, who was credited with 18 aerial victories in 17 days during World War I.

To support the increased naval presence in the Pacific area, the Ford Island Naval Air Station was commissioned in January 1923. A seaplane hangar and other facilities were built on the southeastern side of the island.

During the 1930s, the dredging of Pearl Harbor produced enough landfill to enlarge the 334-acre island to 441 acres, and both Army and Navy facilities were expanded. But the island proved to be too small for both services and the Army transferred its operations to the newly developed Wheeler Field.

On March 20, 1936, the island was in the news as the site of Amelia Earhart's crash-landing during her attempted round-the-world flight.

In 1939, as the result of growing American concern over its defenses, many of the present steel and concrete buildings were built on Ford Island. The base was used for overhaul and repair of most of the Pacific Fleet planes and as a supply base.

The initial Japanese attacks were aimed at knocking out the planes at the naval air station to ensure that the battleships around the island could be attacked without harassment from the air. Nine enemy dive bombers took part in the attack on Ford Island itself. The most severe damage was to Hangar 6 and its seaplane ramp at the southeast corner of the island. Pounded by at least five bomb hits, the hangar and many nearby planes were soon afire. The northeast corner of the structure was burned to its steel framework, and the seaplanes were charred wrecks. There was some damage to the ramp and to Hangar 38.

A delayed action bomb apparently intended for the moored USS *California* slammed into the courtyard of the dispensary and exploded 20 feet beneath the ground, caus-

ing much damage but no casualties. Electrical, water and steam services to the building were disrupted.

When the USS *Arizona* blew up at its Ford Island moorings, the ship settled on the 12-inch main water supply pipe to the island and crushed it. A six-inch line at the south end of the island was damaged at the Navy Yard side, cutting off that supply. A pump was installed on an artesian well on the island to provide enough water to fight fires. Water from the island's elevated tank had to be rationed.

There was some damage to other buildings from misdirected bombs and fragments from exploding ships. Pilings at the small boat harbor and elsewhere were damaged by the oil fires on the water.

The USS *Neosho*, a navy tanker, had just finished discharging aviation gasoline to the tanks on the island when the Japanese planes arrived. Disregarding their own safety, the fueling detail removed the hoses from the tanker and cast off her lines, enabling the ship with its highly volatile cargo to clear the pier and avert a possible disaster.

Emergency first aid stations were set up in the mess hall, the Marine barracks and the new bachelor officer's quarters to augment the dispensary facilities, which could not handle all the 200 wounded from the ships. After the attack, the casualties were evacuated across the harbor to the naval hospital. Several thousand sailors from the bombed and sinking battleships, many covered with oil, eventually made it to the island and were given food, clothing and shelter in many buildings and homes.

Of the 70 planes at Ford Island, 33 were destroyed or damaged. At no time either during or after the attack was the naval air station out of commission. Only one individual was killed and 25 received minor injuries.

Capt. J. M. Shoemaker, Commanding Officer, NAS Ford Island, March 15, 1941, to June 8, 1942.
USN

View of Ford Island in 1925. The Army's Luke Field is to the west (left) and the Naval Air Station, commissioned in January 1923 is to the east (right). The Navy took full control of the island in November 1939 when the Army moved all its facilities to Hickam Field. NA

Seaplane base and Hangar #6 on the southeast end of Ford Island on March 5, 1926. Many of the larger aircraft, including one in the water, are Curtis F5L Flying Boats. Four of the smaller aircraft on the ramp are Martin SC-1 torpedo-bombers. USN

The Army airfield, Luke Field, on Ford Island in 1924. Operations were moved to the new Wheeler Field in the 1930s. HA

Extension of the Seaplane Beach with Hangar #6, May 11, 1934. USN

An early day view of Ford Island showing newly constructed fuel tanks. Some of the water area to the right was eventually filled in. Battleship Row is to the right. HA

This northerly view over Ford Island on Oct. 10, 1941, shows the various naval aircraft facilities situated here at the time. On the west shoreline (left) are the utility aircraft hangars. Across the airstrip (known previously to the Army Air Corps as "Luke Field"), and at lower center of photo, are the patrol squadron hangars which housed the PBY aircraft of PAT-WING-2. The first bombs to fall on Dec. 7 would destroy the large hangar #6 in the foreground. NA 80-G-279375

In this overhead view of Ford Island on Nov. 10, 1941, five battleships as well as the *Lexington* can be seen at their offshore moorings. The *"Lex"* at berth Fox-9 was, by a stroke of good fortune, at sea transporting 18 Vought scout bombers of Marine Scout-Bombing Squadron 231 to Midway Island. She would ultimately meet her fate in May 1942 at Coral Sea. NA 80-G-279385

NA12/A12-1A16

JMS-10-ram
Jan. 25, 1942

War Diary of U.S. Naval Air Station, Pearl Harbor, T.H.

Sunday, 7 December, 1941

Holiday routine

0740 U.S.S. *NEOSHO* completed discharging aviation gasoline to Naval Air Station, and back pressure taken to clear fuel lines.

0750 Aircraft observed approaching Ford Island from the general direction of Merry Point and Hickam Field, but were not identified as Japanese carrier-based planes until the parking area and hangar #6 were bombed, followed by torpedo and bombing attacks on the ships of the fleet moored around Ford Island.

0757 General Quarters sounded, and word of the attack put out on all available radio and teletype circuits.

Hangar #6 set ablaze by bomb hit on eastern end and surrounding parking area damaged by five bomb hits, the largest producing crater approximately 20' in diameter by 7' deep, VP and VO-VS planes in the area destroyed or damaged by fire, fragments, and machine gun bullets. A delayed action bomb apparently intended for the U.S.S. *CALIFORNIA* at berth in Fox-3 exploded under the court of the dispensary, disrupting electrical, water and steam service to this building, but caused no injury to personnel.

Except for this initial attack on the seaplane area, none of the subsequent enemy attacks appeared to be directed at the Air Station, but fragments from A.A. projectiles, and from bombs exploding on or near ships moored around the island, machine gun bullets and 1.1 projectiles fired from the ships in the harbor, together with machine gun fire from enemy aircraft fell on the station, particularly around waterfront areas throughout the attacks. Fragments from the *ARIZONA* explosion were blown generally over the northeasterly end of Ford Island. Three delayed action bombs intended for Battleships at Berth Fox-5 and Fox-6 fell in open areas near those berths and exploded harmlessly underground.

When *ARIZONA* blew up at Berth Fox-7, she settled on the 12" water main, crushing it, and cutting off all fresh water to the Air Station, as the 6" temporary line at the south end of the island was cut off at the Navy Yard (presumably damaged). This necessitated strict rationing of water, despite the installation of a pump on the artesian well near building 167, to provide for the fire and flushing systems.

Oil fires caused damage to the fueling pier at Fox-4, where the fueling detail, Ensign D.A. Singleton, A-V(S), U.S.N.R., A.L. Hansen, C.M.M. (PA), U.S.N., and A.C. Thatcher, A.M.M.2C, U.S.N., with disregard of personal safety and with devotion to duty, ignoring enemy bombs and machine gun bullets, removed the hoses from the *NEOSHO*, cast off her lines, enabling her to clear the pier, and opened the sprinkler valves to the tanks. Other fires caused damage to the dock house, the face of Landing "A" and Berth Fox-1½.

Emergency first aid stations were set up in the mess hall, marine barracks and new Bachelor Officer's Quarters, where, together with the dispensary, about 200 wounded received medical attention. Casualties were evacuated to the Naval Hospital as soon as raids subsided. Air Station boats performed exemplary service in rescuing personnel from the waters of the harbor. Several thousand refugees from *ARIZONA, WEST VIRGINIA, OKLAHOMA, CALIFORNIA, UTAH* and other ships were given food, clothing and shelter.

0900 War Plan #46 put in effect against Japan.

1100 Last air raid ended, but personnel remained at general quarters, and preparations for repelling renewed enemy attacks continued. Station security increased preparations made for blackout.

Blackout at sunset.

2000 Air raid alarm sounded. Six *ENTERPRISE* planes attempting landing on Ford Island were fired upon by all units in Pearl Harbor; four planes lost.

Injuries to Naval Air Station personnel this date: Killed in action, CROFT, Theodore W., A.O.M.1C, USN (VP-21); 25 persons received minor injuries from burns or flying debris.

8 December, 1941

0230 Fire started by embers from burning battleships in vicinity of C.P.O. quarters; extinguished.
0245 fire broke out at landing "A"; extinguished at 0300.
0515 Air raid alarm; no attack. Continued salvage operations and preparing suitable defense facilities. Evacuated battleship personnel to Receiving Barracks. Blackout.

9 December, 1941

Continued salvage operations, improved station security.
1120 Battery "F" of the 251st Coast Artillery, Capt. C.L. Ogden, U.S.A. Commanding aboard for duty. Blackout.

Hangar #6 burning with some intact PBYs in front. The OS2U "Kingfisher" to the left foreground was lifted by crane off of the sinking *California*. Two OS2Us got airborne that afternoon. Both flew despite damage sustained. One crashed near Barbers Point. USN

Looking over the wrecked aircraft at Hangar #6 on Ford Island, the destroyer *Shaw*'s forward magazine has exploded, sending a huge plume of fire and smoke skyward. USN

Bob Barrigan, shown here with his wife, is the sailor standing with his back to the camera on the left. His story follows on the next two pages.

Fast Action And A Lucky Break

On Friday, Dec. 5, 1941, I was assigned to a detail consisting of two other men and myself—one was Holden AMM 1/c. I can't remember the other. We were to take our two OS2U aircraft to Ford Island and remain with them until our ship the *Tangier* AV8, came back in. All, or most of the ships, including ours, was to go out to sea Saturday on maneuvers.

We went to Ford Island and were quartered in the transient bunkroom. I believe the other person with us was a first class metalsmith named Ingleman. Anyway, we all went into Pearl saturday evening, did some shopping, and I went to a PTA dance. We returned to Pearl Harbor and back to the barracks about 10:30-11:00 p.m.

Sunday morning I was awakened by a large explosion which shook the bunkroom. I jumped up as I felt a second one and ran to the window. We were on the second floor facing Diamond Head. I looked over our swimming pool down toward the No. 1 Hangar, and I could see large billows of smoke coming from it. My first thought was that one of our PBY patrol craft had hit it coming in. I then felt several other smaller explosions and saw an aircraft crossing low in the hangar area from south to north banking around and climbing. It had large red balls on the wings. I shouted to the others the Russians were attacking us.

We put on our white pants, shoes and hats and ran downstairs. As I came down the stairway, I couldn't believe my eyes—men had brooms and sticks and were breaking out all the glass frames in the doors and windows. I did not have time to dwell on it because a boatswain's mate got me and several others and ordered us to follow him. We went out the door to the street, and he shouted for us to keep low and follow him. We did, running up the street past the swimming pool. Aircraft machine gun tracers were going past us, and we could hear explosions and glass breaking. He led us to the armory. It was also very hectic there—people were opening up all kinds of ammunition boxes, rifles, gas masks, etc.

An old Chief grabbed me, threw two belts over my shoulder, a rifle and a gas mask and told me and another seaman to go up on the roof of the Operations Building. I remember running all the way over there and running up the narrow stairway to the roof. The roof was about 20′×30′ as far as I can remember; also, there was a wall around it about 24″ or 30″ high. There was a small permanent shed which held cleaning material. We ran to the side of the shed and looked around. It was an unbelievable sight. Except for the area in front of us, we had a view of everything up to the fuel dumps and the hospital on the hills. Planes were coming all across the water from the Navy

Yard area. They would fly low, 50′ to 100′ over the water, drop bombs and torpedoes on the *West Virginia, California, Arizona*—all the battleships on that side; fly directly over us strafing—do the same to the *Tangier, Utah, and Raleigh*; then make a high turn over Beckoning Point and the Pan Am base and return. I saw only two aircraft hit and go down.

During this, the seaman and myself loaded our rifles and watched the waves of aircraft coming. As they approached, we would go behind the shed, fire at them as they passed directly overhead, run to the opposite side and repeat the same firing. I do remember telling the seaman I was with that we could have done better with hand grenades because the planes were so low I could see the pilot and man in the rear seat very plain. At some period during the early time on the roof, two Marines came up and uncrated a box, set up a Browning watercooled machine gun in about 2 minutes and fired it without water until the barrel was so hot the tracers were corkscrewing out.

From that point I saw the *Nevada* get under way and try to move out. I saw the destroyer *Shaw* get a direct hit and exploded. I saw the *Oglala* roll over, many whaleboats and captain's gigs got strafed, people burning in the water, and the ferry getting strafed. I saw bombs being dropped on the *Arizona*. I did not see it hit but felt the explosions.

At some period of time two men came up and told us we were relieved to go down to the mess hall to eat and be reassigned after we calmed down. We both noticed we had red marks over our right side arms and face. We did not know what the red marks were. All we had on were pants and skivvy shirts (undershirts). Our ears were also ringing and the roof deck was covered with small pieces of paper. The battleships were just below us. The *California* was laying sideways and had been firing its large guns at an angle to us. I believe what caused the red marks on us were the shell waddings hitting us during this time, but we were unaware of it.

Anyway, I don't remember the time, but I left the roof, kept my rifle, what ammunition I had left, and my gas mask. I made my way over to the messhall where I was relieved of my rifle and ammunition but kept my gas mask. I remember being in line at the mess hall, not really hungry but in line because I was told to eat. I looked around me but did not see anyone I knew. I saw men in everything I could think of. Dirty clothes, shorts to Admiral's coats, some wounded. The whole scene was unbelievable then as it still is now. I really became sick and frightened for the first time when I looked back against the mess hall— and under the tables were several rows of dead men. When I got to the head of the line with my tray, the cooks were apologizing for the cold chicken. Because the *Arizona* had set on the main Ford Island watermain, we were drinking the swimming pool water. This was later confirmed and guards were posted around the swimming pool. Anyway, when I looked at the cold chicken, orange juice, and dead men I left the mess hall without eating. And to this day, I still cannot eat cold chicken.

I was put in a truck and taken down to the hangar area. I went over to where our two aircraft were parked—in front of the second hangar from the one that had a direct hit. No more than three or four hours had past. I guess it was after 11 or 12 o'clock. Everything was burning—aircraft parts and chunks of concrete were everywhere. When I approached our area, I saw our two aircraft and the two men I came off the ship with on detail by the aircraft. Holden was sitting on the ground and Ingleman was near the wing.

Holden got me and said we were trying to get one of our aircraft flyable. One had a large chunk of cement through the right wing so we were going to take off one wing and place it on the other aircraft. All of the damage was from chunks of cement. We went into the hangar to see if we could find space to put the aircraft. I noticed that two incendiary bombs had come through the hangar roof and never exploded, but had thrown yellow powder all over the aircraft.

That night I was put on a .50-caliber gun crew to help load ammunition by the hangar. During the day we had several false alarms of new air raids and we always ran to the runway area where a trench was dug for some reason. We all jumped in there till it was clear.

That night on the gun crews, with guys from the other ships, was my worst time. As it grew dark, we became more apprehensive since the rumors were that the Japanese transports would be landing at night and air raids were expected prior to that. What all gun crews were told was that if an attack was imminent condition red would be indicated by the fire station who would sound a continuous blast. So we waited; it got dark; it was very quite; and we were nervous. I had to rest my knees against the sandbags to keep them up. Sometime, I don't know just what time it was, but we heard aircraft coming in up the channel from the direction of Diamond Head; their formation lights were blinking; we didn't know what they were. Suddenly, some ship out in the bay near the dry docks opened fire just for a few minutes; then every gun in the Pearl Harbor area joined in. You couldn't even hear a yell and not even a bird could have survived. The tracers lit the sky, several aircraft were hit. I saw them go down burning—one to the south and two on up the hill toward the Navy hospital. We sadly later learned they were F4Fs from the *Enterprise*. No one slept that night.

The next morning—second day—we went back to work on our aircraft. The Executive Officer of Ford Island came by and told us that he wanted us to notify our ship's captain that we would be working around the clock on the aircraft. I was elected to go. I made my way back to the quay where the *Tangier* was docked. I went up on the quarter deck and spoke to Capt. C.F. Spraque. I repeated to him the message. I cannot repeat what he said—but, in no uncertain terms, he told me to get the rest of the men, forget the aircraft, and be back on the ship within a half hour. We came back.

We moved out in the bay the next day. After that a lighter came alongside, and for two days and nights loaded ammunition, guns, bombs, aircraft parts and about 100 marines. We left about Dec. 15 and met a task force—*Saratoga*, destroyers and other cruisers. We never really knew where we were going. One afternoon and the 2nd or 3rd day we all were circling. What happened was that a destroyer had been refueling from the *Saratoga* and had gotten its crossmast hooked into the walkway around the *Saratoga*'s stack. We could see them working with cutting torches—after dark—I believe we lost several hours. The next day we steamed steady. I had every four hour fantail watch to watch the distance of the ship directly aft. I went off watch about 12 midnight and went back on at 4:00 a.m. I looked at the compass and noticed we were going in the opposite direction, and most of all, we had only one ship, the destroyer *Blue* with us.

We ended up going to Midway Island. This was funny— we stopped outside for the pilot—took him aboard and proceeded into the bay. We picked up a tug just inside the bay and he put a steel line on our fantail—we proceeded in. The dock was several hundred yards to our port ahead. We were to make a hard left turn and the tug was to assist pulling us hard to increase the turn.

We started our turn fast, too fast to throw off the tug line. We were pulling the tug sideways. Our 1st Lieutenant cut the wire with an ax and we went about 20 feet up the center of the dock tossing civilian workers and their bags in the water on each side of the dock. They had been waiting for us to take them back to Pearl Harbor.

What we later found out was that our ship was to reinforce Wake Island. Captain Sprague had orders to run the ship aground to assist the Marines if we did not have time to unload. Because of the coral reefs they had to use a donkey engine and lighter to get supplies ashore. So because of the problem with the destroyer and the *Saratoga* refueling episode, that delay most likely saved the *Tangier* crew because Wake Island was taken over by the Japanese during that time.

BOB BARRIGAN
1441 SW 68th
Oklahoma City, Oklahoma 73159

A burned-out section of Hangar #6, a few days after the attack. The structure was damaged by at least five bombs, the largest producing a crater 20 feet wide and 7 feet deep. A sandbagged gun emplacement was established on the ramp. USN

Hangar #6 was abandoned years ago and torn down in the late 1980s.

Oil and debris from the bombed battleships washed up on the east shore of Ford Island. Note the shack and the H-shaped structure where the dredge pipeline meets the shore. This is the Ford Island ferry slip, which is still in use today. NA

Smoke from burning fuel oil obscures the battleship *California* moored at Fox-3 opposite the Headquarters Building, Ford Island. NA

Cleanup has already begun at the Seaplane Base on Ford Island. Smoke at center is from the destroyer *Shaw* in YFD #2. Toward the right rear can be seen the fore and aft masts of the *Nevada*. AMC

Re-arming clips and belts on Ford Island. NA 80-G-32497

In a hastily set up bunker, a .50-caliber machine gun crew, awaits a follow-up attack by enemy aircraft, possibly on Dec. 9. This view is looking west across a sea plane ramp to Beckoning Point and Middle Loch. Note two TBD-1 Devastators parked on left. The two men without helmets are probably survivors from one of the sunken ships. NA 80-G-32543

Machine gun emplacements such as these along the ramp on the south end of Ford Island proliferated in the wake of the Japanese attack on Dec. 7. Curtiss SOCs from cruiser-based VCS units are in the background, along with a pair of PBYs, one of which (visible behind the hangar at right) has its engines warming up. *Nevada*, beached off Waipio Point, is in the background (left), visible beyond the three SOCs. NA 80-G-324-92

The dispensary as it looks today.

Lt. Comdr. Art Humphries in the courtyard of the Ford Island dispensary, where a Japanese bomb exploded.

Dispensary on Ford Island that was hit by a delayed action bomb probably intended for the *California* Berth Fox-3. It landed in the inner court and exploded, causing slight structural damage to the building and cutting electrical, water and steam services. No one was injured.

Smoke still billows from the stricken *Arizona* in this northeasterly view taken a day after the attack from the highest point on Ford Island, the control tower atop the water tower. Aircraft below include Sikorsky JRS-1's and Vought OS2U's. New utility hangar still under construction can be seen in right foreground. USN

Scene at the Seaplane Base following the attack. Several PBYs are parked near a burned hangar. In the left background is the beached *Nevada*. NA 80-G-32505

A wrecked seaplane. This is all that remains of a Vought OS2U-2 Kingfisher observation plane destroyed on Ford Island during the attack. AMC

View of the abandoned airfield on Ford Island in 1981. At one time, Ford Island was the site of the Army's Luke Field as well as the Naval Air Station. There are plans for the eventual demolition of the field and unused support facilities, to make room for much needed housing for military personnel stationed at Oahu. Plans also include a causeway or bridge, possibly from Aiea to Ford Island, thus eliminating the ferry.

Buildings on Ford Island.

I was to be second-in-command of a flight of six F4F-4 fighters from the **U.S.S. Enterprise** that were to escort 19 torpedo planes and six scout planes on our way to find the Japanese Fleet, which a report said had been located.

Unfortunately, the report was erroneous, as we later found out. However, we were launched and went out some 200 miles.

It was dark when we returned to the ship and my flight leader talked to the **Enterprise**, and asked for permission to land. The ship said, "Hell, no. We're not going to light up for you. Go into Pearl Harbor," and gave us a coded direction.

We turned on the heading toward Pearl. Everything was blacked out except burning ships, which we thought were burning cane fields. It was 8:30 Sunday night.

As we passed Diamond Head we turned toward Ford Island in a loose formation and were given permission to land. Most of our gauges had been indicating we were running out of fuel for the last 20 minutes.

When we broke formation in preparation for landing, everything in Pearl Harbor opened up on us with their anti-aircraft batteries. The sky was ablaze with gun tracers.

Lt. (j.g.) Fritz Hebel, the squadron commander, took off towards Wheeler Field but was shot down and killed when he tried to land. Ens. Herb Menges crashed and was killed at Pearl City. Ens. Gayle Hermann's plane took a 5-inch shell through his engine, and spun in right on the Ford Island golf course. He survived. Ens. David Flynn bailed out over Barbers Point and we found him 10 days later at Tripler Army Hospital with a broken leg. Ens. Eric Allen was killed by a 50-caliber machine-gun bullet after parachuting from his crippled plane.

I called the Ford Island tower and told them I was coming in. I put my wheels down and headed back right over the harbor about 50 feet over the water.

I roared right past the foretop of the **Nevada**. They turned all their guns on me but nothing connected.

Moments later I touched the runway. I overshot. There were two crash trucks in front of me at the end of the runway. I slammed on the brakes and spun around in a full circle on the first green of a golf course just beyond the field.

I taxied back up the field. A Marine gunner sprayed the plane with bullets. He just missed my head.

Of the six planes and pilots I was the only one to land intact; three others were killed.

After this frightening experience, I went to the BOQ to find a bed. I could see and hear the **Arizona** still burning. I wanted to call my wife who was staying east of Pearl City but assumed that with all the damage around that there would be no telephone service. I picked up the phone anyway, and to my surprise got a dial tone. To my complete surprise I dialed my number and got through to my wife.

I was the luckiest man in the Navy on Dec. 7, 1941.

Capt. Jim Daniels, Ret.
Kailua, Hawaii

An F4F-4 carrier fighter. This was the type that flew into Ford Island from the *Enterprise* on the night of the attack. USN

The Fleet

The Pride of the Navy

Prewar sailors on the Waikiki Beach.

Lewis Saunders was an officer stationed on the *New Orleans* at the time of the attack. He now lives in San Diego, Calif.

Dear Mother,   December 11, 1941

There isn't very much that I can say right now except that I am all right — but I suppose that that covers the point in which you are mainly interested at the moment.

I know that it is silly for me to tell you not to worry — but please do try to worry as little as possible about me. I'm all right now and I intend to stay all right. The second thing I want you to remember is this: don't worry if you don't hear from me. I need hardly say that the mail situation is pretty uncertain right now.

With love,
Louis Saunders.

(use same address as before — but omit mention of my rank.)

The *Raleigh*, a light cruiser, was built by the Bethlehem Steel Co., Quincy, Mass., and commissioned Feb. 6, 1924. In the opening minutes of the attack Dec. 7 she was hit portside, amidship by a torpedo from the *Soryu* Air Group. The ship began to list rapidly and it was feared she might capsize, but valiant damage control efforts of her crew saved the ship. *Raleigh* earned three Battle Stars in WWII. She was sold for scrap at Philadelphia in February 1946. USN

The light cruiser *Phoenix* was commissioned Oct. 3, 1938, at the Philadelphia Navy Yard. The ship luckily, was not damaged in the attack. She would go on to earn nine battlestars for her wartime service. At war's end she was decommissioned and placed in the reserve fleet. She was transferred in 1951 to Argentina and renamed *General Belgrano* in 1956. She was sunk by the submarine HMS *Conqueror* on May 2, 1982, during the Falkland Island War with Great Britain. USN

St. Louis, the "Lucky Lou," was built by the Newport News Shipbuilding and Drydock Co. and was commissioned May 19, 1939. The ship was docked outboard of *Honolulu* at the Navy Yard for overhaul on Dec. 7. Undamaged during the attack, she moved away from the pier at 0931 and headed for South Channel and the open sea. As the ship cleared the harbor entrance, a midget sub fired two torpedoes that just missed and exploded on a coral reef 200 yards from the *St. Louis*. Decommissioned June 20, 1946, she was transferred to the Brazilian Navy on Jan. 29, 1951 and renamed *Tamandare*. She was stricken in 1975. USN

Shaw was commissioned Sept. 18, 1936, and was in the floating drydock for repairs along with the yard tug *Sotoyomo*. *Shaw* took three bomb hits at about 0910 and blew up in a spectacular explosion at 0930 that also sunk the *Sotoyomo* and the drydock. *Shaw*'s stern structure was salvaged and fitted with a temporary bow. On Feb. 9, 1942, she steamed to the West Coast for a complete rebuilding. *Shaw* earned 11 Battlestars and was scrapped in 1947. USN

The *Allen*, last of the Pre-World War I destroyers, was recommissioned Dec. 9, 1940. She joined the *Ward* *Chew* and *Schley* to form Destroyer Division 80 based at Pearl Harbor. *Allen* was moored between the *Chew* and the ex-*Baltimore* at Buoy X-Ray 5 in the East Loch and was not damaged in the attack. *Allen* would operate in the Hawaiian area for the duration of the war until she was scrapped in 1946. USN

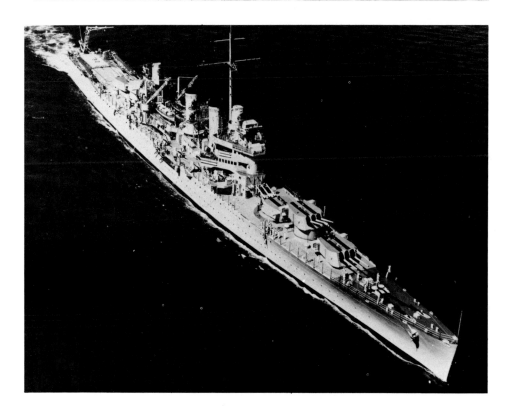

The *Honolulu*, the "Blue Goose," was built by the New York Navy Yard and commissioned on June 15, 1938. During the Dec. 7 attack she suffered severe flooding from her hull as the result of a near miss by a 250 kg. bomb that exploded less than 20 feet away. She was repaired by Jan. 12, 1942, and would go on to earn eight Battlestars and a Navy Unit Citation. She was decommissioned Feb. 3, 1947, at Philadelphia and sold for scrap in 1949. USN

Monaghan (DD-354), with Lt. Cmdr. William P. Burford in command, was the Ready Duty destroyer on Dec. 7 and got underway at 0827 hours. As the ship proceeded down the west side of Ford Island, the *Curtiss* signaled the destroyer of the presence of a submarine in the harbor. *Monaghan* rammed the sub and dropped two depth charges, sinking the intruder. *Monaghan* was lost on Dec. 18, 1944, when she capsized in the fury of typhoon "Cobra" off the Philippines. USN

Downes (DD-375) was on blocks alongside the *Cassin* (DD-372) in Drydock #1, forward of the *Pennsylvania*. At 0902 *Soryu* dive bombers began the second wave strike against Drydock #1 with two 250-kg. bomb hits. The *Downes* was virtually destroyed by three 250-kg. bombs. Vital machinery and equipment was all that could be salvaged. These would be installed in a new hull and by November 1943, the resurrected *Downes* was ready for sea duty. USN

Whitney, a destroyer tender, was built by the Boston Navy Yard, and commissioned on Sept. 2, 1924. On Dec. 7, she was moored at Anchorage X-ray 8 in East Loch. She was supplying steam, electricity and fresh water to her nest of ships of Destroyer Division Six, the *Conyngham* DD-371, *Tucker* DD-374, *Case* DD-370, *Selfridge* DD-357 and *Reid* DD-369 tied up alongside. These ships opened fire at the attacking aircraft by 0804. The *Whitney* was scrapped in 1948. USN

The *Neosho* (AO-23), a large fleet oiler, arrived at Pearl Harbor on Dec. 6, 1941, to offload a cargo of high octane aviation fuel at the Naval Air Station, Ford Island. Luckily, the ship was not hit during the attack. Her explosive cargo would have posed a more serious peril to the already devastated ships of Battleship Row. *Neosho* was with Task Force 17 at the Battle of the Coral Sea and was sunk by enemy aircraft on May 8, 1942. USN

Curtiss, a large seaplane tender, commissioned Nov. 15, 1940, was moored off the entrance to Middle Loch. At 0836 she spotted a midget submarine and commenced firing. The sub launched a torpedo that missed the *Curtiss* and hit a dock at Pearl City. *Curtiss* scored a direct hit with her 5-inch gun through the sub's conning tower. The destroyer *Monaghan* finished off the sub a few minutes later. USN

The *Helena* hoisted her commission pennant at the New York Navy Yard on Sept. 18, 1939. She was assigned to the Pacific Fleet in 1940. On Dec. 7 she was moored at the Navy Yard's 1010 Dock, a berth normally assigned to the battleship *Pennsylvania*. Three minutes into the attack, the *Helena* was hit amidships by a single torpedo that passed underneath the minelayer *Oglala* that was tied up alongside. The ship did not sink and continued firing her antiaircraft guns until the attack was over. The *Helena* was lost on the night of July 6, 1943, in the Battle of Kula Gulf during the Solomon Islands campaign. EA

Avocet (AVP-4), a small seaplane tender, was moored on the east side of Ford Island at the Naval Air Station dock (near Fox 1A). She opened fire immediately. An early round from her 3-inch, .50-caliber antiaircraft gun scored a hit on a Japanese torpedo plane attempting to evade after launching a torpedo at the *California*. The aircraft burst into flames and crashed in the vicinity of the Naval Hospital. EA

The *Tern* (AM-31), a "Bird" Class minesweeper of World War I vintage, was moored at the end of 1010 Dock inboard of the yard oiler YO-30. Able to get underway by 0943, *Tern* moved into the harbor and rescued 47 men from the oily waters. She then fought fires continuously on the blazing *West Virginia* and *Arizona* for the next 48 hours until the fires were under control. USN

Moored at the Coast Guard Base in 1941 at Honolulu was the CG-8, a former rumrunner of the prohibition era. Astern of her is the USCG *Kukui*, a buoy tender. The Coast Guard Base was not bombed by the Japanese attackers. EA

The *Pelias* (AS-14) was originally the *S.S. Mormacyork*, a C-3 freighter for the Moore-McCormick Steamship Lines. The ship was acquired by the U.S. Navy for conversion to a submarine tender and was the Navy's newest ship at Pearl Harbor having commissioned on Sept. 5, 1941. Tied up at the sub base, the ship was not damaged during the attack. *Pelias* was sold in 1971. USN

The *Rigel* of 1922, a repair ship, was berthed at the Navy Yard repair basin for an extensive refit and conversion. On the day of the attack her superstructure was incomplete and covered with scaffolding. Her crew, unable to fire at the attackers because there was no armament on board the vessel, assisted other ships in rescue and salvage work. *Rigel* received minor damage and returned to service on April 7, 1942. USN

Japanese Midget Submarines

The Objective Was Not Accomplished

Ens. Kazuo Sakamaki's abandoned Type A midget submarine aground at Waimanalo Bay, approx. 600 yards from Bellows Field, about 40 miles from Pearl Harbor on the morning of Dec. 8. Ens. Sakamaki's sub was one of five that formed the "Special Attack Unit." They were transported to within 10 miles south of Pearl Harbor, each secured to the deck of a fleet-type mother submarine. They were released at midnight on Dec. 6-7 and would attempt to gain entry through the nets protecting the harbor entrance. USN

The most bizarre element of the Pearl Harbor attack was the use of midget submarines. They were employed, despite the skepticism of several Japanese admirals, in the hope that they could damage inner-harbor ships that the attacking planes missed. As it turned out, the mini-subs constituted Japan's only failure in the remarkably successful surprise attack that crippled the United States fleet.

Having experimented with midget submarines since the 1930s, the Japanese Navy had developed them well enough to convince Yamamoto himself to employ five in the Pearl Harbor attack. Five I Class submarines, the largest in the Japanese fleet, were hastily fitted to carry the midget Type A subs aft of their conning towers in piggyback fashion. The group was designated the Special Attack Unit.

Since the midgets were driven by small electric motors with short-lived batteries, they had to be launched close to their targets. Eighty feet long, six feet in diameter at their widest point and displacing 46 tons, each boat carried two 18-inch torpedoes and was controlled by a two-man crew. Top speed was 23 knots on the surface, 19 knots submerged.

On Nov. 25, 1941, five I Class submarines and their attached midget subs left Kure Naval Base for the Hawaiian Islands. Slowed by their 46-ton cargo, the group did not follow the carrier strike force route to the north, but instead set a direct course for Pearl Harbor.

The larger submarines were to approach within 10 miles of Pearl Harbor, fan out before the entrance and launch their midget submarines early on the morning of Dec. 7. The mother boats would then retire west of Lanai Island where they would pick up the midgets that returned from the attack.

For their part, the midgets would penetrate Pearl Harbor, sail counterclockwise around Ford Island and launch

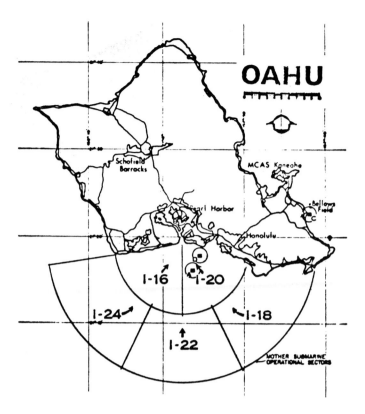

Operational sectors of the five I-Class submarines around the entrance to Pearl Harbor at the time of the attack.

their torpedoes at the capital ships when the air attack began.

From the moment of launching, nothing went right.

Because of an inoperative gyrocompass, the midget from I-24 lost its way, drifting around the other side of Oahu and finally beaching itself on a coral reef off Bellows Field on the night of the 7th. Ens. Kazuo Sakamaki, the submarine's commander, attempted to blow up his boat, but it was captured intact. Both crewmen tried to swim ashore,

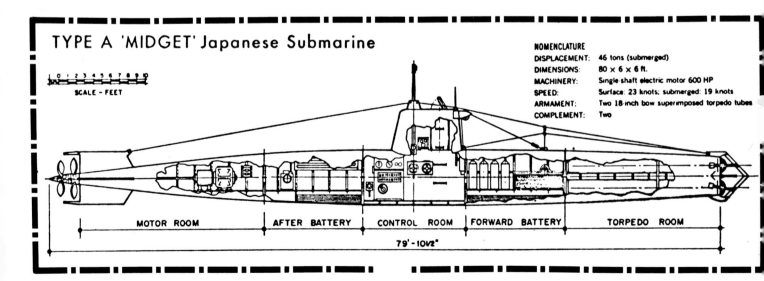

TYPE A 'MIDGET' Japanese Submarine

SCALE - FEET

NOMENCLATURE
DISPLACEMENT: 46 tons (submerged)
DIMENSIONS: 80 × 6 × 6 ft.
MACHINERY: Single-shaft electric motor 600 HP
SPEED: Surface: 23 knots; submerged: 19 knots
ARMAMENT: Two 18-inch bow superimposed torpedo tubes
COMPLEMENT: Two

| MOTOR ROOM | AFTER BATTERY | CONTROL ROOM | FORWARD BATTERY | TORPEDO ROOM |

79' - 10½"

but only Sakamaki made it. He was captured—America's first Japanese prisoner of the Second World War.

Another midget was sighted outside the harbor by the destroyer U.S.S. *Ward* one hour before the air attack. Shelled, depth-charged and sunk in 1,200 feet of water, the little sub became the first Japanese casualty of the Pearl Harbor attack.

One midget did penetrate the harbor and was sighted by the seaplane tender U.S.S. *Curtiss* after the air attack had begun. The submarine launched a torpedo at the *Curtiss*, but it missed the tender and instead struck a dock at Pearl City. The sub also fired a torpedo at the U.S.S. *Monaghan*, which was racing to clear the harbor, but the shot missed and the destroyer rammed, depth-charged, and finally sunk the Japanese boat. It was raised after the attack and used as fill material for a new pier at the submarine base at Pearl.

The fourth midget was apparently sunk outside the harbor by depth charges after she fired torpedoes at the U.S.S. *St. Louis.* In 1960, she was accidentally discovered by Navy SCUBA diver trainees and brought to the surface by the U.S.S. *Current.* Because no human remains were found inside the boat, it was surmised that the crew might have escaped alive, swam to shore and assimilated into the Japanese population on Oahu.* The boat later was transferred to the Japanese Navy and is now on display at the Maritime Self-Defense Force Service School at Eta Jima, Japan.

The last midget is presumed to have been sunk outside the harbor on the 7th or 8th. Several American destroyers reported attacking enemy subs on those days.

Thus, all five midget submarines and their crewmen were lost. The Special Attack Unit inflicted no damage on the American fleet.

---

*There has been no evidence to prove this supposition.

Nine of the midget submariners who attempted to attack Pearl Harbor painted on silk by an unknown Japanese artist. The tenth, Kazuo Sakamaki, was stricken from Japanese records and officially ceased to exist. Names, left to right were: PO 1/c Yoshio Katayama, PO 1/c Naoshi Sasaki, PO 1/c Shigenori Yokoyama, Sub. Lt. Masaji Yokoyama, Lt. Naoji Iwasa, Sub. Lt. Shigemi Furuno, Ens. Akiro Hirowo, PO 2/c Sadamu Ueda and PO 2/c Kioshi Inagaki. USN

Coming Soon!

CAPTURED
2-MAN
JAP SUB

SEE YOUR NEWS-
PAPERS★LISTEN TO
YOUR RADIO FOR
LOCAL DETAILS ★

The sub was brought to Wilmington, Del., on April 1943.
DELAWARE STATE ARCHIVES

Ensign Kazuo Sakamaki's captured midget submarine on display in New York City's Times Square for a war bond drive. The submarine toured cities in 41 states around the country to help sell war bonds for America's war effort. It was mounted on a trailer and had 22 small windows installed around the hull with two mannequins dressed as Japanese sailors inside. EA

HA 19, America's first war prize, on temporary exhibit at the Admiral Nimitz Museum State Historical Park in Fredricksburg, Texas (1991). After its capture the sub was put on display at Subase Pearl Harbor and then taken to the mainland where it spent the war years touring the country, promoting war bond sales. At the end of the war it wound up in Chicago and eventually was sent to the submarine base in Key West, Fla. In 1964 it was put on display at the Lighthouse Museum in Key West. In 1991, it was moved to the Admiral Nimitz Museum. It will be placed on permanent display at Pearl Harbor in the future.
ADMIRAL NIMITZ MUSEUM

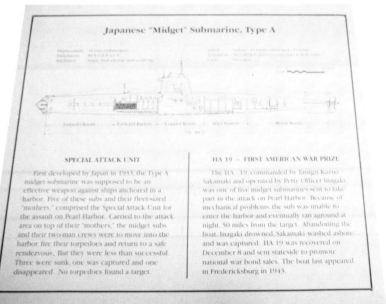

Japanese "Midget" Submarine, Type A

SPECIAL ATTACK UNIT

First developed by Japan in 1933, the Type A midget submarine was supposed to be an effective weapon against ships anchored in a harbor. Five of these subs and their fleet-sized "mothers," comprised the Special Attack Unit for the assault on Pearl Harbor. Carried to the attack area on top of their "mothers," the midget subs and their two-man crews were to move into the harbor, fire their torpedoes and return to a safe rendezvous. But they were less than successful. Three were sunk, one was captured and one disappeared. No torpedoes found a target.

HA 19 — FIRST AMERICAN WAR PRIZE

The HA 19, commanded by Ensign Kazuo Sakamaki and operated by Petty Officer Inagaki, was one of five midget submarines sent to take part in the attack on Pearl Harbor. Because of mechanical problems, the sub was unable to enter the harbor and eventually ran aground at night, 50 miles from the target. Abandoning the boat, Inagaki drowned. Sakamaki washed ashore and was captured. HA 19 was recovered on December 8 and sent stateside to promote national war bond sales. The boat last appeared in Fredericksburg in 1943.

Haliewa Field, July 4, 1941.

Ewa Marine Corps Air Station, Oct. 1, 1941.

Kaneohe Naval Air Station, Oct. 1, 1941.

Bellows Field, Oct. 1, 1941.

P 36s of the 6th Pursuit Squadron at Wheeler Field. They were ferried to Hawaii by aircraft carriers and later repainted in olive drab.
HARRY BROWN

Nine SBD-2s and -3s of Scouting Six over the Pacific on a tactics hop. Oct. 27, 1941. 6-S-14 an SBD-3, nominally assigned to Ens. Edward T. Deacon, VS-6's engineering officer, would be shot down by American antiaircraft fire from Fort Weaver. NA

P-40 fighters over Hawaii in August 1941. USAF

(O-233.4-917-C-18)(8-1-41-9:00A)(12-200) P-40 FORMATION, OAHU, T.H.

B-18 bombers on the flight line at Hickam Field. By the time of the attack these planes were obsolete. HA

These P-36 fighters are shown at the 1939 Cleveland Air Races in various paint schemes. Some of these planes probably ended up stationed in Hawaii in 1941. USAF

A Navy PBY-5 "Catalina." These planes flew regularly out of Oahu on patrol duty. Most were destroyed on the ground at Ford Island or Kaneohe Naval Air Station in the initial stage of the attack. NA

Sikorsky JRS-1 utility amphibian, the "One-Jig-One" of Utility Squadron One (VJ-1) was one of 10 JRS-1s based at the Naval Air Station, Ford Island, in 1941. Powered by two 750 h.p. Pratt & Whitney "Hornets," she cruised at 166 mph with a range of 775 miles. On the afternoon of Dec. 7, the 1-J-1 flew a five-hour mission in search of the Japanese carriers. John Birmingham relates that he flew as a gunner/crewman with a 30-0-6 rifle looking for enemy fleet. The pilot was Lt. James Robb. NA 80-G-463233

The "One-Jig-One" is one of the surviving aircraft (in original condition) that was present during the attack. It is currently on display at the storage facility of the National Air and Space Museum in Silver Hill, Md.
ROBERT BRACCI

two years later. Even now, the ambiguity in the citation awarding me a medal for action that day has plagued me. I've always attributed the delay to the fact that my medal was awarded to Harry "M." Brown and whoever inverted that middle initial from the correct "W." rendered me into two different people in a world where someone with a name like Harry Brown has a constant fight to escape anonymity. I really don't care so much for myself since I know what I did that day and whether my total is recorded as six or seven won't significantly affect anything. However, for the record, a radio transmission which was initiated to consolidate my records with the Seventh and Fifth Air Forces gives me credit for two (General Order No. 193, Hq Fifth Air Force, APO 925, 10 Sept. 1943). Moreover, that it was accepted by my peers is a demonstrated testimonial which I also received from the C.O. when I was to return to the States. He confirmed my total as seven. Also, I would have been hoorawed off the field when I painted two rising suns on my P-40 in Hawaii if there had been any doubt on the part of my associates.

Recently, students of that event have asked about the coloring of the Japanese aircraft engaged. I can only give impressions for I have no definite memory. I believe that each of the two for which I claim credit had a blue belly band, and one of them had a single yellow or orange stripe, raked, on the vertical stabilizer. Both were Kates although my Form 5 records them as Vals.

I returned to Haleiwa and landed. A servicing crew chief teasingly pointed to how I was dressed. Only then did I realize that I had flown my first combat mission dressed in pajama tops, tux trousers, houseshoes, and helmet and goggles! While the airplane was serviced, I changed into a flight suit. Taylor and Welch took off on another search. About five minutes later Johnny Dains taxied out in a P-36

Harry Brown passed away in late 1991.

and I gave him a thumbs-up as he taxied by. That was the last time I saw him alive because, as he was hurrying to join Taylor and Welch, our own ground troops opened up and shot him down! I suppose all that excited people could see was that his P-36 differed in appearance from the P-40s he was trying to catch! I flew one more brief mission that day without seeing any action.

HARRY W. BROWN

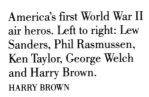

America's first World War II air heros. Left to right: Lew Sanders, Phil Rasmussen, Ken Taylor, George Welch and Harry Brown.
HARRY BROWN

I Won't Be Back

Following the destruction of the P-40s on the ramp at Wheeler, I saw many dead in the base barracks and tent areas. Some had attempted to escape the strafing by digging through wooden tent floors with their bare hands. Hands and fingers were lacerated, and in many instances finger nails torn out. It was a poignant sight.

Only one fighter of my 46th Squadron had been damaged, and I proceeded to get my P-36 and three others into the air. I had selected three veteran pilots, but when we were in the air I noticed that one was a young inexperienced pilot who somehow had taken over a plane.

In a slight dive at near maximum throttle we sighted a formation of 11 enemy fighters headed north, and came in at an overtaking speed from about level flight. Firing at the leader, I watched my tracers enter the fuselage, saw him pull up slightly and then fall off to the right, smoking, I also saw one of our planes hit, and spiral toward the ocean, trailing smoke. Later, when we returned to Wheeler, Lt. Rasmussen, Lt. Thacker and I were shot at by our own ground personnel who thought we were the enemy, but we managed to land safely. Rasmussen's plane was pitted with 54 elongated holes from 20-millimeter fire, both on the wings and the fuselage. It appeared that a heavy axe had been used to make them.

During the debriefing I learned that Lt. Norris, one of the pilots I had originally selected for the mission, had returned to the parachute truck for a smaller chute when young Lt. Sterling, who had been standing nearby with chute and life vest, jumped into the waiting plane. Sterling handed his wristwatch to the crew chief with instructions to have it sent to his mother because he wouldn't be back. It was his plane I saw spiraling into the ocean.

The price was high when one considers that this single action cost us a pilot and two planes, in exchange for three confirmed and one probable enemy plane losses. Although acceptable in this particular context, it also illustrated the cost of being unprepared.

All the pilots received Silver Stars for their gallant action that day.

COL. LEWIS SANDERS, USAF, Ret.,
Lillian, Alabama

(A lieutenant at the time of the attack, Sanders is credited with shooting down one of the first Japanese plane of the minutes-old war.)

HAWAIIAN AIR FORCE AS OF DEC. 7, 1941***

TOTAL STRENGTH
754 officers, 6,706 enlisted men.

CASUALTIES	KILLED	MISSING	WOUNDED
HICKAM	121	37	274
WHEELER	37	6	53
BELLOWS	5	0	9
TOTAL	163	43	336

PLANES

AIRCRAFT	TOTAL	DESTROYED	USABLE
B-17D	12	4	4
B-18A	33	12	11
A-20A	12	2	5
P-40C	12	5	2
P-40B	87	37	25
P-36A	39	4	16
P-26	14	0	14
TOTAL	223****	64	77

***Courtesy--Office of Information, 15th Air Base Wing (PACAF) Hickam AFB, Hawaii
****Plus an assortment of observation and training planes.

Ken Taylor is retired and living in Anchorage, Alaska.

JAPANESE AIRCRAFT TYPES USED IN THE PEARL HARBOR ATTACK

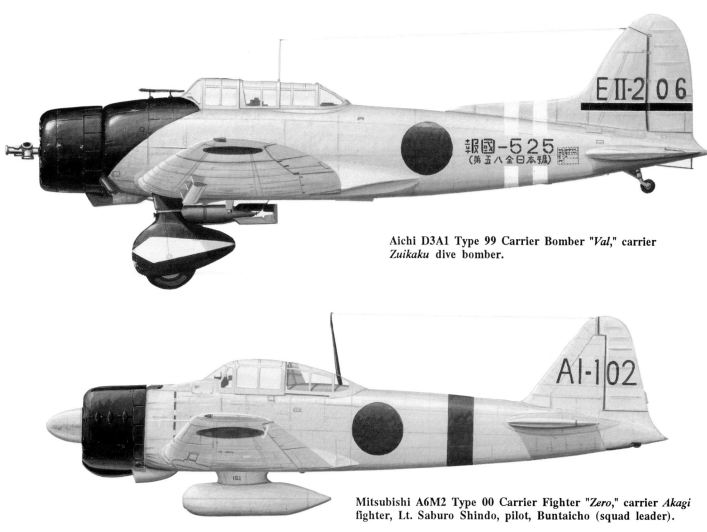

Aichi D3A1 Type 99 Carrier Bomber *"Val,"* carrier
Zuikaku dive bomber.

Mitsubishi A6M2 Type 00 Carrier Fighter *"Zero,"* carrier *Akagi*
fighter, Lt. Saburo Shindo, pilot, Buntaicho (squad leader).

Nakajima B5N2 Type 97 Carrier Attack Plane
"Kate," carrier *Hiryu* torpedo bomber. Lt.
Hirata Matsumura, pilot, Buntaicho.

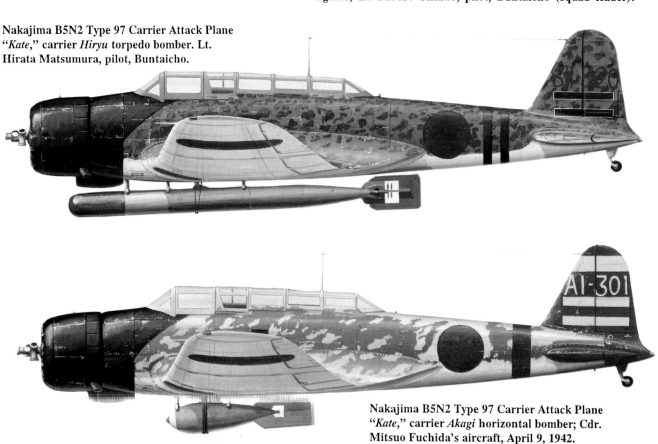

Nakajima B5N2 Type 97 Carrier Attack Plane
"Kate," carrier *Akagi* horizontal bomber; Cdr.
Mitsuo Fuchida's aircraft, April 9, 1942.

AMERICAN AIRCRAFT PRESENT DURING THE PEARL HARBOR ATTACK

Curtiss P-36A flown by 2nd Lt. Philip M. Rasmussen from the 46th
Pursuit Squadron, Wheeler Field.

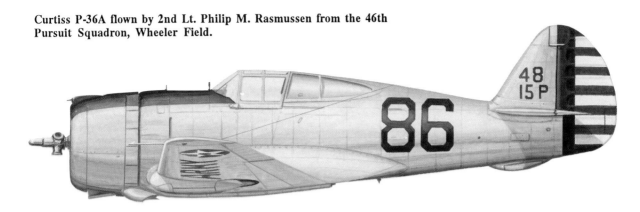

P-40B *Tomahawk* from the 47th Pursuit Squadron, Haleiwa Field.

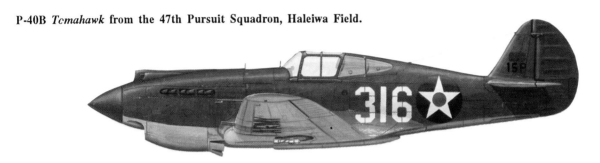

SBD-3 *Dauntless* flown by Lt. Clarence E. Dickinson from VS-6, *USS Enterprise*.

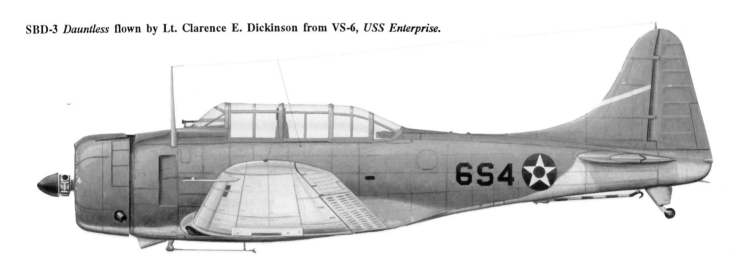

B-17C *Flying Fortress* flown by Lt. Robert H. Richards. Arriving
inbound from California during the attack, Lt. Richards made a
forced landing at Bellows Field.

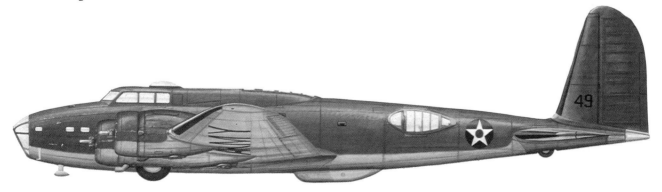

Aichi D3A1 Type 99 EI-204 piloted by Lt. (jg) Iwakichi Mifuku. This plane attacked Hickam Field in the first wave.
MICHAEL WENGER

A damaged second wave fighter. The Japanese lost 20 aircraft in the last attack. NA 80-G-19931

A navy photographer took the closest photo of an attacking Japanese dive bomber. NA 80-G-33013

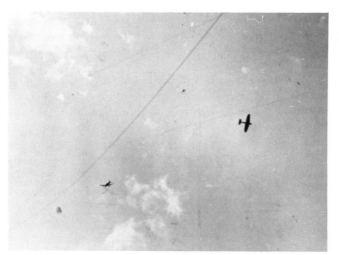

Three Aichi D3A1 Type 99 "Val" carrier bombers from the *Kaga* attack the battleship *Nevada*. This photo was taken from Ford Island. NA

Japanese Airmen Killed or Missing In Action During the Attack*

Nagaaki Asahi	*Kaga* D3A II
Shunichi Atsumi	*Soryu* A6M II
Toshiaki Bando	*Kaga* D3A II
Hajime Goto	*Akagi* D3A II
Ippei Goto	*Kaga* A6M II
Toru Haneda	*Kaga* A6M I
Takeshi Hirano	*Akagi* A6M I
Fumio Hirashima	*Kaga* D3A II
Kinsuke Homma	*Akagi* D3A II
Fusata Iida	*Soryu* A6M II
Fukumitsu Imai	*Kaga* D3A II
Tomio Inenaga	*Kaga* A6M II
Saburo Ishii	*Soryu* A6M II
Kunio Iwatsuki	*Shokaku* D3A I
Satoru Kawasaki	*Soryu* D3A II
Hirokichi Kinoshita	*Akagi* D3A II
Syuzo Kitahara	*Kaga* B5N I
Isamu Kiyomura	*Hiryu* D3A II
Kenichi Kumamoto	*Kaga* B5N I
Tetsusaburo Kumazo	*Shokaku* D3A I
Hideyasu Kuwabara	*Soryu* D3A II
Kazuyoshi Kuwabata	*Kaga* D3A II
Yoshiharu Machimoto	*Kaga* B5N I
Saburo Makino	*Kaga* D3A II
Kenji Maruyama	*Soryu* D3A II
Yoshizo Masuda	*Kaga* B5N I
Isamu Matsuda	*Kaga* B5N I
Tsuneo Minamizaki	*Kaga* D3A II
Tsuneki Morita	*Kaga* B5N I
Hajime Murao	*Hiryu* D3A II
Izumi Nagai	*Kaga* B5N I
Shigenori Nishikaichi	*Hiryu* A6M II
Nafikatsu Ohashi	*Kaga* B5N I
Iwao Oka	*Kaga* D3A II
Shigenori Onikura	*Kaga* D3A II
Toshio Onishi	*Kaga* B5N I
Seiichi Ota	*Akagi* D3A II
Toshio Oyama	*Akagi* D3A II
Noboru Sakaguchi	*Kaga* D3A II
Kiyoshi Sakamoto	*Akagi* D3A II
Seinoshin Sano	*Kaga* A6M I
Chuji Shimakura	*Akagi* D3A II
Yoshio Shimizu	*Kaga* B5N I
Yoshio Shimizu	*Hiryu* D3A II
Koreyoshi Sotoyama	*Hiryu* D3A II
Shigeharu Sugaya	*Akagi* B5N I
Sueo Sukida	*Kaga* D3A II
Mitsumori Suzuki	*Kaga* B5N I

Ryochi Takahashi	*Soryu* D3A II
Hidemi Takeda	*Kaga* B5N I
Tomoharu Takeda	*Kaga* B5N I
Nobuo Tsuda	*Kaga* D3A II
Yonetaro Ueda	*Kaga* B5N I
Nobuo Umezu	*Kaga* B5N I
Doshi Utsuki	*Akagi* D3A II

*Includes their carrier, type of aircraft and if they were in the first or second wave.

Lt. Shoichi Ogawa of *Kaga*'s dive bomber aircraft. He lost his two wingmen during his attack on the *Nevada*. USN

An Aichi D3A1 Val noses over with dive brakes in use.
NA 80-G-32708

One of two *Kaga* dive bombers shot down in Wahiawa city limits, just outside Wheeler Field. AMC

This *Kaga* torpedo bomber, AII-356, flown by Lt. Mimori Suzuki crashed in the waters of the southeast loch of Pearl Harbor. USN

This Val is another *Kaga* loss. This crash was used by U.S. technical intelligence. The *Kaga* lost four Zeros, five Kates and six Vals, more than any other Japanese carrier that day. NA 80-G-32441

This Akagi Zero, AI-154, crashed into the Fort Kamehameha ordnance building killing the pilot and three soldiers. NA 80-G-13040

Sam Tooney, a sugar cane plantation executive, points out to radio announcer Ken Carney the tail section of a Japanese dive bomber that crashed in a macadamia nut grove and exploded. HA

Other pieces of the plane came down nearby. HA

A corpse of a Japanese airman is raised from his downed aircraft after several days in the water. His face was eaten by crabs prior to recovery. NA 80-G-32465

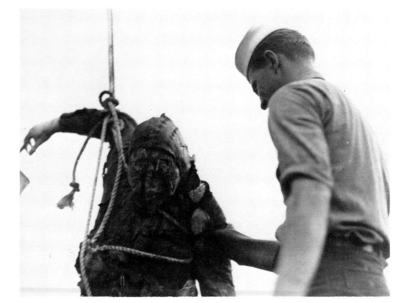

The tangled wreckage of a Japanese plane is wrapped around a tree. NA 80-G-32567

The body of a Japanese airman is retrieved from the oily waters of Pearl Harbor. NA 80-G-32553

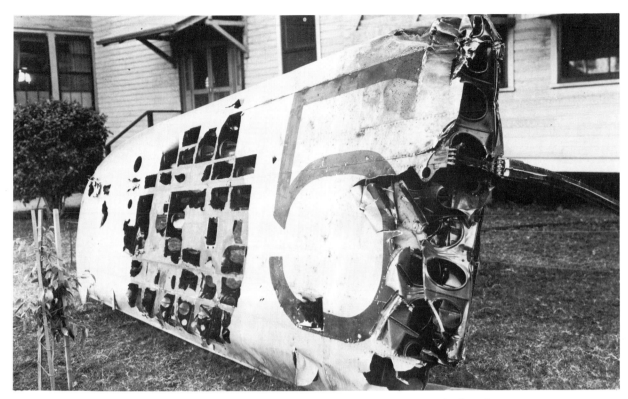

This *Kaga* torpedo plane crashed near the Pearl Harbor base hospital. The first plane to crash, the wing section was stripped for souvenirs soon after the attack was over. The tail code can only be reconstructed thus far to read AII-35x, the last digit is unknown. FORREST SMITH

A Japanese plane retrieved from the waters of Pearl Harbor. USN

Aerial view taken Oct. 13, 1941, of Southeast Loch with many fleet subs in port at the submarine base (right) and the fleet supply depot on Kuahua (center). Across the top, looking toward Pearl City and Aiea, are the north end of Ford Island, Battleship Row and the fleet anchorage in East Loch. NA 80-G-411193

The Japanese fleet moves into final position during the night of Dec. 6, 1941. Sailing a northern route and maintaining complete radio silence, the six carriers and their escorts arrived undetected in Hawaiian waters. PAUL BENDER

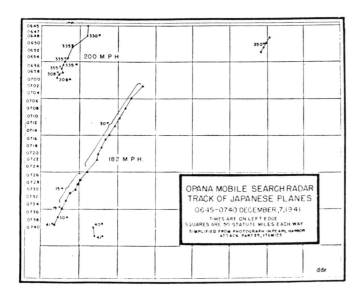

OPANA MOBILE SEARCH RADAR
TRACK OF JAPANESE PLANES
0645-0740 DECEMBER 7, 1941
TIMES ARE ON LEFT EDGE
SQUARES ARE 50 STATUTE MILES EACH WAY
SIMPLIFIED FROM PHOTOGRAPH IN PEARL HARBOR
ATTACK PARTES, ITEM 23

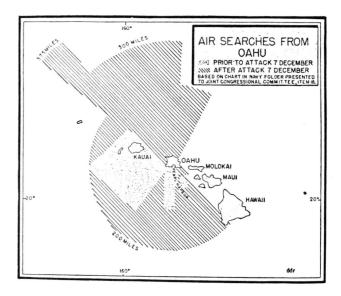

AIR SEARCHES FROM OAHU
PRIOR TO ATTACK 7 DECEMBER
AFTER ATTACK 7 DECEMBER
BASED ON CHART IN NAVY FOLDER PRESENTED
TO JOINT CONGRESSIONAL COMMITTEE, ITEM 18.

View looking northeast across West Loch to Ford Island in the opening minutes of the attack at approximately 0758. The destroyer *Helm* has just rounded Waipio Point. At extreme left, the *Utah* has taken a torpedo hit; center, the large plume of smoke is burning Hangar #6 on Ford Island and right center, smoke from torpedo explosion on the *Helena*. EA

The *Shaw* was in the floating drydock for overhaul. She burned furiously from three 250kg aerial bomb hits. This photo was taken before 0930, only minutes before her forward magazines blew up in a fiery explosion. USN

One of the most dramatic photos of World War II is the explosion of the U.S.S. *Shaw* in the floating drydock YFD #2. The *Shaw* was hit by three 250-kg. bombs that were meant for *Nevada*. One passed through the bridge, igniting fires and rupturing fuel tanks. The blazing oil fires caused the forward magazine to explode in a fiery blast that tore the ship's bow off. The *Nevada* with the tug *Hoga* is on the right. USN

The *Shaw*'s forward magazines erupt in a fiery blast, sending smoke and flame hundreds of feet into the air. The *Nevada* had swung around (right) after running aground at Hospital Point. At the left, the garbage lighter YG-21 pulls in behind the *Avocet* at the NAS Pier on Ford Island. USN

At 1010 dock men from the capsized *Oglala* set up a first aid station and mounted four .30-caliber machine guns on the dock that were saved from their ship before she rolled over. The *Helena* is just ahead of *Oglala*. To the right is the burning *Shaw* in the floating drydock YFD-2.
NA 80-G-464887

Late on the morning of Dec. 7, with her bow and bridge area completely destroyed by the explosion of the forward 5-inch ammunition magazine, the *Shaw* lies in the sunken floating drydock, YFD-2. On the right is the listing battleship *California* and the civilian dredge *Turbine*. The port side of the sinking yard tug *Sotoyomo* YT-9 can be seen in the lower left of the drydock. NA 80-G-19939

Looking southwest toward Ford Island and the Navy base, across the cane fields of Aiea. Smoke billows from Hickam Field and Battleship Row from the devastation wrought by the Japanese Air Armada. USN

This view, taken around 0926, shows two nests of destroyers alongside their tenders. In the center of the photo are (left to right), *Dobbin* (AD-3), with *Hull* (DD-350), *Dewey* (DD-349), *Worden* (DD-352) and *MacDonough* (DD-351) alongside. The ship to the left of the nest is *Phelps* (DD-360), which got underway on two boilers around 0926. The other nest consists of (left to right), *Whitney* (AD-4), *Conyngham* (DD-371), *Reid* (DD-369), *Tucker* (DD-374), *Case* (DD-370) and *Selfridge* (DD-357). *Solace* is barely visible at far left. NA 80-G-33045

Pearl Harbor as seen from Aiea shortly after the last planes of the Japanese First Air Fleet left the scene of their shattering victory. Columns of smoke rise thousands of feet into the late morning skies from the havoc wrought by the attackers. In the foreground are a pineapple processing plant and surrounding pineapple fields. The *Vestal* (AR-4) is aground on Aiea Shoals (right). NA 80-G-32893

Looking toward the Navy Yard area from the north end of the Marine Barracks Parade Grounds. The late morning skies are filled with towering clouds of smoke from the carnage wrought at Battleship Row. A 3-inch antiaircraft gun is being set up in the foreground expecting the attackers to return. The center water tower is the Pearl Harbor signal tower. It was from here at 0755 that the blue signal flag for "prep" was raised prior to the raising of morning colors at 0800 on all ships and stations in the harbor. USN

View of the Marine Barracks Parade Grounds at the Pearl Harbor Navy Yard between 0930 and 1030. The skies have been darkened by billowing clouds of black oily smoke from the crippled ships of Battleship Row. Joe Ciampi, 3rd Defense Battalion USMC of Ocala, Florida, sits in the foreground. Twelve Marines gathered in circles with their Springfield '03 rifles waiting for another attack. USN

Destruction

The Enemy Achieved Complete Surprise

Aerial view of Battleship Row on Dec. 10, 1941. The sunken *California* is at upper left. In the center is the capsized *Oklahoma* with *Maryland* inboard, followed by the sunken *West Virginia* alongside *Tennessee*. The *Arizona* is at lower right. Fuel oil is still leaking from the shattered hulls. NA 80-G-387565

Shortly after the attack, salvage work on the beached *Nevada* is underway. The *Widgeon* (ASR-1), a salvage vessel, is alongside, left. The divers and crew of *Widgeon* would earn a commendation from Admiral Nimitz for their successful efforts in helping to refloat the *Nevada*. NA 80-G-32452

The *Vestal* was beached off Aiea landing. Note damage and scorched paint on the aft section caused when she was moored alongside the *Arizona* when it blew up. USN NH 50273

The *Arizona* on the morning of Dec. 9, with her main decks awash, fires are still smoldering amidships. Entombed forever within shattered remains are the bodies of approximately 900 of her crew. USN

A work party had just finished rigging awnings on the *Arizona*'s quarterdeck for morning church services before the first bombs fell and mortally wounded the ship. Lt. Cmdr. Samuel G. Fuqua was the senior surviving officer and from his station on the quarterdeck he directed firefighting and the removal of wounded. When he realized the ship could not be saved, he gave the order to abandon ship. His coolness and bravery under such extraordinary conditions earned him the Medal of Honor. USN

BOTTOM PHOTO, PAGE 152.
Several days after the attack, fires are out on the sunken *West Virginia* and just aft, the *Arizona*. When the *West Virginia* settled on the bottom, the inboard *Tennessee* was wedged against the quays, which had to be partially dismantled to free her. The *Tennessee* was finally freed on Dec. 16 and sailed for the West Coast on Dec. 20, 1941. USN

Two yard oilers are tied up (photo, left) alongside the sunken *West Virginia* to recover fuel oil still remaining in her bunkers prior to the start of salvage work. When the *West Virginia* settled on the bottom, the inboard *Tennessee* (photo, lower left) was wedged against the quays, which had to be partially dismantled to free the ship. The *Tennessee* was finally freed on Dec. 16, 1942, and the *West Virginia* was refloated and put in drydock on June 9, 1942, for repairs. USN

On the overcast morning of Dec. 8, the minesweepers *Bobolink* (left) and *Vireo* (right), along with the water barge YW-10, are moored to the stern of the sinking battleship *California*. USN

The crew of the *California* and the rescue craft, alongside, are pumping out water-filled compartments and removing fuel oil in an attempt to lighten the ship and prevent it from settling on the bottom. The salvage vessel to the right is the *Widgeon*. USN

-153-

On the morning of Dec. 7, the editor of the *Honolulu Star-Bulletin*, Riley N. Allen, found himself with the most momentous story in local history and the greatest exclusive of his life, owing to a press breakdown at the *Honolulu Advertiser*, the *Star*'s competitor and the city's only Sunday newspaper. Allen's hastily recruited staff issued three extras that day. The first was printed fewer than two hours after the attack. HA

Japanese Photos
Great Propaganda Value

This photo shows fire of the six Japanese attack force carriers, taken from the deck of the *Akagi* in Hitokappu Bay in November 1941. Aircraft on board are four TYPE 99, Model 11 "Val" bombers. Large carrier to the left is the *Kaga*, the two distant ones are the *Shokaku* and *Zuikaku*. To their right is the *Hiryu* and out of sight to the right is the *Soryu*.

The *Akagi* (top) and *Kaga* (bottom), Japanese carriers of the First Carrier Division. USN NH 73059, 73060

The *Hiryu* (top) and *Soryu* (bottom), Japanese carriers of the Second Carrier Division. USN NH 73063, 73061

The *Zuikaku* (pictured) and the *Shokaku* made up the Fifth Carrier Division. USN NH 73069

Capt. Koji Shiroshime of *Shokaku* stands before a blackboard which stated: "Japanese Imperial Fleet! You must obey and die for your country, Japan! Whether you win or lose, you must fight and die for your country!" NA 80-G-182248

Airmen prepare for their epic flight. USN

One of the eight fleet oilers that made up the support force.

View of the *Akagi* shipping water over the bow en route to Hawaii. Photo taken from above the starboard boat stowage deck (forward).

View taken from the *Zuikaku* with the *Akagi* in the lead and the *Kaga* following.

View from the *Akagi*'s stern. Directly behind is *Kaga* and to her rear is *Hiryu*.

Flight deck of the *Akagi*. Visible are two A6M2 "Zeros" (one is AI-110) and three B5N2 "Kate" bombers with green upper surface camouflage paint.

Flight crews rush to their planes on the *Shokaku*.

AA gun practice aboard *Akagi* at Hitokappu Bay (Kurile Islands) in November 1941 before departing for Hawaii. Gun in the foreground is an aircraft Type 92. 7.7 mm (copy of the Lewis) used in the rear position of the "Val" and "Kate" aircraft. Some flight crew members look on.

This remarkable series of Japanese photos is courtesy of the University of Hawaii via the U.S. Army Museum in Honolulu.

Attaching bomb splinter padding to *Akagi*'s island bridge. Aircraft is an A6M2 "Zero" with quilted engine cover.

On board the *Agaki*. The aircraft is a A6M2 Model 21, Type O Carrier fighter (Zero). Note the splinter padding on the island and an AA machine gun fitted on top. The rope coil by the range finder provided splinter protection but also could be played out for abandoning ship. The crew is being briefed in the background for the second wave attack. The Zero shown is AI-101 piloted by Petty Officer 1st Class Tadao Kimura. It was the second plane launched in the second wave.

Shokaku crews receive instructions.

The Type 91 modification 2 torpedo.

Photo taken aboard *Akagi* in May 1942 during filming with training unit of B5N1 Kates for the Japanese movie *Hawai Marei Oki Kaisen*. NA 80-G-182245

Air group leader Cmdr. Mitsuo Fuchida was navigator on this Kate high-level bomber. March 1942.

A Val taking off from the *Zuikaku* by a Shotaicho (flight leader). The plane is the 58th gift from Japanese people as noted by the inscription on the fuselage side. AM

Blackboard on *Akagi* lists orders for the impending battle. AM

Blackboard on *Akagi* displays a map of the Pearl Harbor area. AM

P01c. Tadao Kimura warms up for takeoff to the left in A1-101. Type 99 dive bomber, Vals warmup in the background. AM1

Shokaku airmen pose on board before their day of destiny. AM

Battle flags waved in the breeze as the fleet left Hitokappu Bay. The top flag is of a two-star admiral. The bottom one is the naval ensign. AM

Lt. Comdr. Tadashi Kusumi, leader of *Hiryu*'s Horizontal bombers. His own flight caused the destruction of the *Arizona*. USN

A "fleet defense" (Combat Air Patrol) Mitsubishi Zero (A6M2) fighter prepares to launch before the Nakajima B5N2 high-level bombers warm up on the flight deck of the carrier *Shokaku*. They are preparing to take off to launch the second attack wave. USN

Flight deck, possibly on the *Hiryu*, showing planes ready for takeoff for the second wave. The Zero in the foreground may be the last of the nine Zeros to launch from the *Hiryu* (it had engine trouble and had to land back on the carrier). The planes in the background are Type 99 dive bombers. USN

The 183 aircraft of the First Attack Group began launching in the gray light of pre-dawn with the first plane lifting off at 0615. Sunrise that morning was 0626 Honolulu time. A torpedo bomber is given the "Banzai" salute by the flight crew of the carrier *Soryu* as it readies for takeoff on the second wave attack. USN

Lee Embree states: "During final approach for landing at Hickam Field, our B-17E, piloted by Lt Karl Barthelmess, was attacked by two Japanese VAL dive bombers. After strafing us from the rear they passed to our left where I took this photo. There was no serious damage to our plane." USAF

The following photos courtesy Lee Embree, Port Angeles, Wash.

"After attacking our plane, these same two VALS turned to the left to return to their attacks upon Ewa Field when another second wave VAL evidently hit by AA fire from Pearl Harbor crashed southeast of Ewa Field. In the foreground is Oahu's south shore near Pearl Harbor's channel entrance." USAF

B-17E in foreground from 38th Reconnaissance Squadron, after arrival from Hamilton Field, Calif. Smoke billowing in right background is from the *Arizona*. B-17D in background is from the 18th Bomb Wing stationed at Hickam. This photograph appeared on the front page of the December 27, 1941, issue of *Life* magazine. USAF

"After landing at Hickam Field, we taxied to a dispersement area and unloaded all available combustible material in case of an incendiary attack by the Japanese aircraft during strafing." The *Arizona* is burning in background. Left to right in photo, assistant crew chief, Sgt. Vance H. Spears and crew chief, T/SGt. Roy H. Coulter." USAF

Hickam Field hangars were badly damaged by Japanese bombs and machine gun fire, which left the buildings and aircraft burning. On right is a badly damaged B-18 airplane. USAF

S/Sgt. Lee R. Embree, at camp site on the edge of Hickam Field. Air crews of the 38th Reconnaissance Squadron were forced to spend the night of December 7 at this site, because the Hickam Field barracks were destroyed. It rained most of the night and there was heavy antiaircraft firing around midnight. USAF

Schofield Barracks & Wheeler Field

Deadly Visitors Wreak Havoc on the Ground

The charred remains of a Curtiss P-40B, one of 83 fighter planes that were destroyed or damaged at Wheeler Field. USA

*S*ituated on the Leilehua Plain almost in the center of Oahu are Schofield Barracks and Wheeler Air Force Base. Both were targets for Japanese planes in the opening minutes of the Pearl Harbor attack.

Schofield Barracks was named after Maj. Gen. John M. Schofield, the prominent U.S. Army officer who helped establish the post. He won the Congressional Medal of Honor during the Civil War, was superintendent at West Point and served as Secretary of War. In 1872, he led a survey party to Oahu and initiated the agreement that gave the U.S. use of Pearl Harbor as a naval base. He was influential in the eventual annexation of Hawaii as a territory in 1898.

The first unit, the 5th Cavalry, arrived at Schofield in 1909, but the construction of the principal barracks and buildings did not begin until 1916. The Hawaiian Division was organized on March 1, 1921, and was stationed at Schofield.

At the outset of World War II, Schofield Barracks was the largest post in the U.S. Army.

Wheeler Field was named on Nov. 11, 1922, in honor of Maj. Sheldon H. Wheeler. He was the commander of Luke Field, on Ford Island, from 1919 until his death in an airplane crash on July 12, 1921.

Construction of the field, which is situated just south of Schofield Barracks, began on Feb. 6, 1922. At the time of the Pearl Harbor attack, it was the largest fighter base in the Pacific area.

The first nonstop flight from the U.S. mainland to Hawaii terminated at Wheeler Field on June 29, 1927, and famed aviatrix Amelia Earhart used the field as her starting point when she made the first solo flight from Hawaii to the mainland on Jan. 11, 1935. Wheeler officially became a separate permanent military post in 1939.

Auxiliary fields were eventually built at Haleiwa on Oahu's northern coast and Bellows on the eastern coast. At the time of the Pearl Harbor attack, some of Wheeler's Army fighters had been dispersed to these coastal airstrips.

On the morning of December 7, Japanese fighters flew to the west of the bases and pounced on Wheeler in an effort to knock out as many of Oahu's land-based fighter planes as possible.

Wheeler Field, May 14, 1931 with Schofield Barracks in the background. HA

Schofield was not attacked with bombs, but by strafing planes. Building 1492 on the west end of the post was one of the first structures hit. Quad C, one of the main barracks, was strafed as was the post library.

But Wheeler Field was the main target. Planes were parked wingtip to wingtip in long parallel lines in front of the hanger.

At 7:51 a.m. the first wave of 25 *Zuikaku* dive bombers bombed and eight *Soryu* Zeros machine-gunned the parked planes for 15 minutes. It was a simple matter for the enemy planes to fly up and down the flight lines, picking off the fighters. The barracks and tent areas and several hangars were just as vulnerable, and were soon in flames.

A second attack, lasting fewer than five minutes, came about 9:10 a.m. Eight *Kaga* Zeros machine-gunned Wheeler fighters as they were taxiing to the runway.

Eleven pilots managed to take off from Wheeler or Haleiwa during two attacks. They claimed 11 enemy planes shot down.

Altogether 83 aircraft of the 153 based at Wheeler were destroyed or damaged; thirty-seven Americans were killed, six were missing and 53 were wounded in two attacks.

Bellows Field on the east coast of Oahu below Kaneohe was established in 1917 as the Waimanalo Military Reservation. It was renamed Bellows Field in 1933, in honor of 2nd Lt. Franklin D. Bellows, an aviator killed in World War I.

An auxiliary base of Wheeler, Bellows had 20 fighter and reconnaissance planes parked in a line at 10- to 15-foot intervals. At 8:30 a.m. a single Japanese fighter machine-gunned the tent area, wounding one. At about 9 a.m. eight *Hiryu* Zeros machine-gunned the parked aircraft, destroy-

ing two fighters and one reconnaissance plane. Two airmen* were killed and four wounded.

Haleiwa Field on Oahu's northern coast was not attacked, although there were a number of planes parked there.

The attacks on Wheeler and Bellows were devastating. Very few fighters were able to get into the air to combat the Japanese fighters, dive bombers and torpedo bombers that were attacking the U.S. fleet at Pearl Harbor. This is exactly what the Japanese had counted on—catching American airpower on the ground.

_____

*2 P-40s shot down on takeoff (1 KIA, 1 WIA), 1 P-40 hit on ground with pilot KIA, 2 P-40s destroyed on ground.

For years, these holes in the wall of Carter Hall, the original post library at Schofield Barracks, were thought to be bullet holes from the attack. This building, however, was not attacked during the raid.

Front view of Funston Gate at the entrance to Schofield Barracks. It was constructed by the 3rd Engineers, Hawaiian Division, in the 1930s. USAMHI

Front view of the south side of Hangar #3 at 1020. Several hangars were badly damaged. USA

The base engineering shops a few days after the attack. It did not take long for military and civilian personnel at all Oahu bases to get back into operation. CAMERA HAWAII/WERNER STOY

A view of the southwest
corner of the machine shop,
completely destroyed
during the attack. AMC

Damage to the gas
engineering building. AMC

Interior view of the
assembly shop showing
damage to windows and
frames. AMC

A TIN HAT WITH NO TOP

On Nov. 19, 1941, at Wheeler Field, Hawaii, final preparations were being made by the 6th and 19th fighter squadrons of the Army Air Corps for departure by aircraft carriers for stations at Midway and Wake islands. The date of departure from Pearl Harbor was set at Dec. 1, 1941.

At that time I was a staff sergeant serving as a flight chief in the 19th fighter squadron. Both the 6th and 19th squadrons were full strength in personnel, planes and equipment.

Excitement was high; the men of the other eight squadrons at Wheeler Field envied us. We expected the Japanese to attack the Philippines but not Hawaii, and for some reason not known to us our departure date was changed to Dec. 8, 1941.

The delay was a great disappointment to us as we felt that perhaps our orders would be canceled, thereby depriving us of getting closer to the Philippines and possible battle.

On Saturday, Dec. 6th, Lieut. Ahola, my flight leader, had flown his plane to Pearl Harbor where it was placed aboard a carrier so that he could practice a take-off to determine the degree of flaps to use. When he returned to the field I decided to place his plane in the hangar for final landing gear check prior to departure on Monday morning. The hangar was completely empty so Lt. Ahola's plane was placed facing out towards the field.

During the past few months we had been on continual alert and ready to fight, our planes dispersed around the field; however, our alert status had changed to protect against sabotage. All planes at Wheeler Field, about 300 of all types, were lined up on the ramps, wing-tip to wing-tip and tail to tail, so as to present as small an area as possible to guard against any possible sabotage.

Sunday, Dec. 7, 1941, started out a beautiful and peaceful day for me. Having finished breakfast with a few other sergeants, I went outside to the road in front of my barracks and waited for the arrival of the paper boy, along with Sgt. Moore and several other early birds.

My thoughts were interrupted by the sound of planes coming through Kolekole Pass. There were three two-engined land planes somewhat resembling our own A-20's, an attack bomber. They were painted olive drab color and as they approached opposite our field they cleared their machine guns

by firing short bursts and continued toward Pearl Harbor. There were no identifying markings on the planes, and as they came abreast of the field our anti-aircraft protection located around the field opened fire with 50 caliber machine guns. I don't know to this day how they knew the three planes were Japanese or why they opened fire as no attack had as yet taken place.

I felt apprehensive but suggested to the group that we go on the ramp and watch what I thought was practice firing. At this time our attention was attracted above us to a squadron of silver planes which were peeling off singly and diving very slowly towards us. I looked toward Pearl Harbor and could see no planes in the air except the three that had come through Kolekole Pass and had headed in that direction. As I looked back to the planes diving at us, the rising sun painted on the wings became visible.

Several comments were made that the Navy was certainly conducting realistic exercises. When the leading plane released two 100-pound bombs, I could see that they were headed for the dump at the end of the hangar line. I just couldn't believe the Navy would drop practice bombs in that area and my heart beat faster as I watched the bombs drop.

When they hit the engineering hangar, the last on the line, all my doubts vanished. Heart beating furiously, I ran into the barracks, up the second floor stairs, all the while shouting, "It's war, men, get to the hangars," my thought being to get to the hangar as I felt sure some of the pilots would do the same and that should be our rightful place of duty.

Men first sat up in their bunks unbelieving. I then ran into my room off the rear porch which I shared with Staff Sgt M. A. Crawford. Crawford was shaving; I didn't say a word, but reached under my bunk, pulled out my pack with the tin hat attached. I couldn't unfasten the helmet so I ran out of the room carrying the pack and tin hat and attempting to unfasten the hat as I ran.

None of the men had as yet reached the stairway and my plan was to get the tin hat on, crawl to the hangar by using the gutter which was about 12 inches deep and get Lt. Ahola's plane warmed up and open the hangar doors. The plane could take off directly to the front between the parked planes.

As I reached the main floor, I noticed a tin hat lying on the hallway floor; how it got there I never found out. I dropped my pack and put on the tin hat, at the same time I was mentally keeping track of the planes attacking us. They were diving between two rows of barracks with the rear machine gunner spraying the barracks to keep personnel away from the planes. At the time I was picking up the tin hat, three planes had passed us, the first plane dropping two bombs and machine gunning. The second dropped no bombs, but machine-gunned and the third passed machine- gunning. I didn't think the third plane dropped any bombs so figured I could continue running to the street, hit the gutter and crawl along it to the hangar.

As I left the shelter of the porch I was looking to my right front and saw Sgt. Guthrie running in the center of the street about twenty yards from me. I got out about five yards from the porch when a bomb hit just about where Sgt. Guthrie was. I didn't hear it, but saw the tree between the bomb and me turn gray and shake. I thought the bomb hit in the tree.

When I regained consciousness I was lying on my stomach and facing toward the barracks, looking at my tin hat with the top cut off. I remember thinking that I must get under cover and getting up on my hands and knees. I then became unconscious for the second time and it was during this period that Sgt Malakowski pulled me into the porch. I got up from the floor while still unconscious and came to just as I was opening the screen door. I did not know then that I had been unconscious a second time. I went to the stairway where the men were lined up to the top floor. I was covered with blood and several men fainted when they saw me. Sgt. S. M. Rackowski was at the foot of the stairs and I instructed him to get the men down on the ground floor, which he did. After the attack was in progress about 15 minutes we had several men wounded. Sergeants Malakowski, Rackowski, and Morgan cleared a space for the wounded and provided first aid; there was no panic and everyone waited for the attack to subside.

My wounds consisted of bomb fragments in the left forearm and left thigh; cement, sticks, stones and other debris embedded over my entire right side and ruptured blood vessels in my lungs. While Sgt. Malakowski administered first aid to me, I attempted to get the men to go to the hangar, thinking that a pilot might have made it to the hangar and would need help to get a plane into the air.

Staff Sgt. Paul Cipreano restrained the men from going to the hangar at this time, and rightly so, due to the entire attacking force concentrating its efforts on the hangar line. Paul said the hangar line and all planes appeared to be on fire and that the Japanese were using 20- millimeter cannon to do the job. As it turned out later, Capt. Morris and Lt. Ahola did make it to the hangar but couldn't have taken Lt. Ahola's plane up as the hangar was under continual heavy enemy fire.

I wondered if the Japanese had landed on our beaches and where the Navy and Marine planes were; everyone was asking the same questions, hoping and praying for the Navy planes to appear, just as the Navy was asking for the Army planes.

Wheeler Field was under attack three times during a period of about 50 minutes. After the enemy planes completed their mission the wounded were assembled on the ground behind the dispensary awaiting transportation to Schofield Barracks Station Hospital. Due to the large number of casualties the hospital staff worked until well after midnight. In my ward we were taken to the operating table on a porch in the order of our arrival, and as a consequence I waited 14 hours to get my wounds attended to and there were two more men after me.

The casualties suffered were high as was the property damage. Out of all the P-40s at Wheeler Field it took an entire week to assemble seven planes from the salvaged parts of destroyed planes.

Initially when we were under attack, I did not see any planes over Pearl Harbor, which leads me to believe that probably Sgt. Guthrie was the first American killed in World War II, and I the first wounded. I have often wondered what course the war with Japan would have taken if our movement to Wake and Midway islands had proceeded as originally scheduled and we had departed from Pearl Harbor on Dec. 1st. We probably would have run into the attacking fleet. Our fighter planes were equipped with bomb racks; perhaps we would not have inflicted much damage, but the defenses of Hawaii would have been alerted to stop the infamous attack.

Maj. George Sallick, USA Ret.
Pensacola, Florida

One of the Army's P-40s destroyed at Bellows Field. USAF

A disabled B-17 at Bellows Field. A flight of B-17s arrived at Oahu from California as the Japanese were beginning their attack. USAF

Ewa MCAS

Bloody Baptism for a New Base

Remains of an SBD Dauntless at Ewa. This view was probably taken sometime after the attack.
W.R. LUCUS, HEALDSBURG, CALIF.

*J*ust to the east of Barbers Point Naval Air Station on the southwestern tip of Oahu Island lies the abandoned runway of what was once the Ewa Marine Corps Air Station.

At the time of the Japanese attack, the Ewa base was not yet a year old. But the history of its use as a military facility dates to the 1930s, when the Navy leased a small piece of land from the Campbell Estate to build a mooring mast for the dirigible *Akron*. However, there is no record that the ship ever moored there.

In early 1940 the Navy acquired 3,500 additional acres from the estate and started construction of an air station for the Marine Corps. The airstrip was completed a year later, and plans were made to develop Barbers Point for naval aviation.

Two minutes before the Japanese attacked Pearl Harbor, one squadron of six Zeros came out of the northwest at an altitude of 500 meters feet and strafed the planes parked on the runway. Descending to within 20 feet of the ground, the enemy planes attacked single aircraft with short bursts of machine-gun fire, then pulled up over the treetops and reversed their course. Soon Vals were screaming in from the opposite direction strafing only.

In all, 33 of the 49 planes stationed at the base were destroyed and 16 damaged. Machinery was put out of commission, installations wrecked, and supplies destroyed.

During a momentary lull, Marines rushed out and dragged unburned planes off the runway. They attempted to mount machine guns on the aircraft to fire back at the attacking planes.

In the midst of the attack, a bright red base fire truck raced out onto the exposed runway toward the burning planes, and was attacked immediately by the enemy aircraft. The driver finally was forced to abandon the truck after machine-gun bullets had flattened his tires. When an officer complimented him afterward for having driven into a hail of bullets, the driver said, "Hell, Lieutenant, I saw a fire, and I'm supposed to put 'em out."

By 9:10 a.m. more Vals and Zeros worked over buildings and undamaged aircraft. As Ewa was near one of the post-attack rendezvous point for the Japanese planes, it presented a convenient target of opportunity for pilots departing the island after completing missions elsewhere.

Shortly after the first attack, six SBD dive bombers from the carrier *Enterprise* landed at Ewa, but were ordered back into the air to keep them from being caught on the ground.

Ewa casualties included four dead and 13 wounded.

Ewa Field, Oct. 27, 1941. NA 80-G451116

Mistaken Identity

*O*n the morning of 7 December, 1941, I was a Marine supply sergeant living with my wife in a small cottage, specially built inside a water tower, overlooking Pearl Harbor We had just gotten up and were expecting guests for a picnic, on the grounds, later that day. Suddenly we saw an explosion over nearby Ford Island. My immediate reaction was a plane had hit the radio tower there during maneuvers; however, upon further examination I realized from the meatball insignia that the planes were Japanese. Both of us immediateiy jumped into our car and headed for our base—the Marine Corps Air Station at Ewa. The only road was repeatedly strafed by enemy aircraft during our journey. Upon reaching the town of Ewa, I dropped my wife off there, with civilian friends, and proceeded on to the base, a distance of approximately one-third of a mile.

Everything there was in a state of chaos. One specific incident: A Marine private by the name of "Lucas" had reportedly been found in the nearby cane fields starting fires in the shape of an arrow, obviously directed toward our base and which could be seen from the air.* He was promptly shot by Marines. I proceeded on with the business involved and did not see my wife for several days. In the meantime, someone (and I am not sure of this—it could have been a civilian worker from the Ewa plantation) indicated Sergeant Lucius had been shot and killed as a spy, this being the only information my wife heard. This obviously was not correct, however, and upon being allowed by my commanding officer, Lt Col Claude A. Larkin to go see her, I assured her that I was alive and in no trouble.

My wife, May, after staying only briefly with our friends in Ewa, assumed a position as a civil service worker at Pearl Harbor. Upon my transfer to Midway Island in early May of 1942, she was evacuated to the United States via the *S.S. Lurline.*

Col. W. R. Lucius, USMC, Ret.
Healdsburg, California

---

*Actually the Marine was Sgt. William Edward Lutschan, Jr., who was eventually buried at the Golden Gate Cemetery, San Bruno, California.

Ewa Marine Corps Air Station was carved out of tropical brush in 1940-41 as the Corps' major base on Oahu.
USMC #145093, 145035, 145047

An unexploded bomb in a cane field after the attack.
USA SC127870

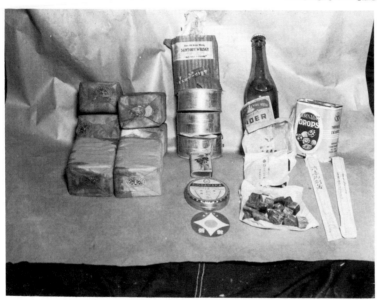

Japanese rations found in a downed plane. NA 80-G-32687

IN MEMORY OF THOSE CIVILIANS WHO
LOST THEIR LIVES IN HAWAII AS A
RESULT OF THE JAPANESE ATTACK
ON HAWAII, DECEMBER 7, 1941
PLACED BY ALOHA CHAPTER F·S·D·A·R·

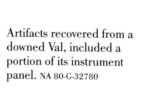

Plaque on the wall of the
Hawaii State Library,
Honolulu.

Artifacts recovered from a
downed Val, included a
portion of its instrument
panel. NA 80-G-32780

Salvage
The Heroes Wore Hard Hats

Forward superstructure and bridge of the *Arizona* on Feb. 17, 1942. Two of her 14"-inch turrets were salvaged from the aft section of the ship to be used as coast defense batteries on Oahu. USN

The Pearl Harbor attack devastated the Pacific Fleet and left U.S. Pacific defenses in shambles. Eighteen ships—300,000 tons' worth—were either sunk or damaged and most of the Oahu-based army and navy aircraft were destroyed or badly damaged.

The Japanese sunk or damaged five of eight Pacific Fleet battleships, thus wiping out the main striking force of the U.S. Navy. Only the aircraft carriers escaped unscathed.

Efforts to rescue trapped sailors from the sunken ships began while the attack was still under way. No one could be rescued from the battleship *Arizona*, which sank quickly, but one Navy man was brought out from the target ship *Utah* through a hole in her upturned hull. Six men were rescued from the capsized battleship *Oklahoma* the next morning after torch-wielding workers cut holes in her steel hull plates. Eleven more were found alive and recovered about noon and 13 more later in the day. In all 32 *Oklahoma* sailors were rescued, the last one on Dec. 9.

In June 1942, when the battleship *West Virginia* was placed in dry dock, the bodies of 20 sailors were found entombed in the ship. Three of them were found in a pump room; messages written on a bulkhead indicated the trapped men had lived until Dec. 23.

Because the Japanese had neglected to bomb the shipyards, yard workers were able to begin repairing the damaged ships almost immediately after the attack. The Navy decided to patch up the ships enough to make them seaworthy, then take them to the West Coast for complete repair, overhaul and refitting. Because the *Arizona*, with 1,102 men entombed in her, was too badly damaged to be refloated, salvage crews removed gun turrets and other components that could be reused. Due to dangerous gases trapped in her hull, the Navy decided not to try to remove the bodies. They were left there as a permanent memorial to the attack victims.

Hundreds of thousands of gallons of fuel oil had to be pumped out of the *West Virginia* before she could be refloated. Her hull patched with 650 tons of concrete, she was raised on May 17, 1942. After undergoing temporary repairs at Pearl, the battleship was sent to Puget Sound Navy Yard for rebuilding. She rejoined the fleet in July 1944 and participated in some of the remaining battles of the Pacific war. Having been patched and pumped out, the battleship *California* was refloated on March 24, 1942. She went to the Puget Sound Navy Yard in October 1942, was rebuilt and rejoined the fleet in late 1943. Salvaging the battleship *Oklahoma* proved to be a massive and time-consuming operation. She had not only sunk but rolled over. First, 350,000 gallons of fuel oil were removed from her hull and a huge air bubble was pumped in to lighten the ship. Twenty-one derrick-like towers were attached to her upturned bottom and connected by cables to 20-ton

winches on Ford Island. Eventually the winch-cable system was able to pull the vessel upright. Owing to the delicate nature of the operation and the shortage of equipment and materials, more than two years had passed before the *Oklahoma* was finally drydocked in December 1943. After the Navy decided that she was not worth rebuilding, her superstructure was stripped and she was sold for scrap. In 1947, while being towed to the West Coast, she sank in a storm, never to be recovered.

Having gone aground at Hospital Point near the entrance to Pearl Harbor during the attack, the battleship *Nevada* had been pulled back off the beach by tugs and had backed across the channel to Waipio Peninsula, where she sank to the bottom in shallow water. She was raised on Feb. 12, 1942, received temporary repairs at Pearl and was restored and modernized on the West Coast. The *Nevada* returned to the Pacific Fleet in time for the Aleutian Campaign, then participated in battles in both the European and Pacific theaters.

The battleships *Maryland, Tennessee,* and *Pennsylvania,* whose damages were not severe, were repaired quickly and returned to service in late 1941 and early 1942. Also sent

Salvage Officer Capt. H.N. Wallin (left) and the Commander of the *West Virginia*, Lt. Comdr. W. White, during salvage operations in 1942. USN NH 64470

into action after quick repairs were three light cruisers, the *Helena*, *Raleigh* and *Honolulu*.

The destroyer *Shaw*, which blew up and sank along with her floating dry dock, was refloated, fitted with a makeshift bow and sailed back to the West Coast in February 1942. Rebuilt, she rejoined the fleet in late 1942.

Although the destroyers *Cassin* and *Downes* were beyond repair, their engines and other machinery were salvaged and shipped to the Mare Island Ship Yard near San Francisco, where new destroyers were built around them.

Considered a total loss, the rolled-over mine-layer *Oglala* was to be dynamited and used for scrap, but the Navy found that it would be just as easy to salvage her as to blow her apart. Refloated in April 1942 and temporarily repaired, she was rebuilt at Mare Island and rejoined the fleet in February 1944.

The *Vestal*, a repair ship, and the *Curtiss*, a seaplane tender, were repaired in 1942 and served in the remaining years of the war.

A stripped-down target vessel, the old battleship *Utah* was not worth the expense of refloating and repairing. Left in the water like the *Arizona*, she is today a memorial to the victims of the attack.

Both Army and Navy airfield were back in operation almost immediately. Repairs were made to bombed-out hangars and other installations within days.

Thanks to the quick action of salvage crews and repair teams, most of the ships damaged at Pearl Harbor eventually rejoined the fleet and took part in the war. On the other hand the Japanese warships that attacked Pearl Harbor would share a grimmer fate. Of the major vessels that participated in the attack, none survived the war. The Imperial Japanese Navy that had once ruled the Pacific was destroyed in the succeeding three and one-half years

The *West Virginia* was raised from her sunken grave in May 1942 and taken to drydock for temporary repairs.

One of the large winches placed on Ford Island, used to salvage the *Oklahoma*. USN SHIPYARD COLLECTION

Looking aft at the beginning of the righting operations on March 8, 1943. USN

Aerial view on March 19, 1943, showing the *Oklahoma* in its 90-degree position. NA 80-G-300131

View looking portside from the *Oklahoma* after the ship was righted. USN

Damage was extensive on the superstructure of the *Oklahoma*. USN

The *Oklahoma* in drydock, 1944. The damage was too severe to consider rebuilding her and she was sold for scrap in 1946. USN

More damage looking aft on the upper deck in the ship's 10-degree position on May 6, 1943. USN

Clinometer on the *Oklahoma* in about the 10-degree position. USN

Fourteen-inch shells being removed through the remains of Turret #4 on the *Arizona*. May 18, 1942. AMC

USS ARIZONA 5/18/42

REMOVING PROJECTILES FROM TURRET #4

CRANE IN BACKGROUND

These views attest to the damage caused by the explosion on the *Arizona*, one of the greatest disasters in U.S. Naval history. USN

Removing the *Arizona*'s superstructure, May 1942. USN

Removal of *Arizona*'s ammunition aft.
Working party equipped for work in
first platform magazines (in face
masks) and on topside (in
respirators), July 1, 1942. USN

U.S.S. ARIZONA   7/1/42

Removal of ammunition aft.
Working party equipped for
work in 1st platform magazines (in face masks) and
on topside (in respirators).

Divers emerge from water-filled
compartments on the *Arizona* in May
1943. Some salvage work was done,
but it was considered too dangerous
to try to recover the bodies of the
men who went down with the ship.
USN NH 64303

Two of the *Arizona*'s
5-inch/51 guns that were
recovered from the wreck.
Tied up across the pier is
the salvaged hulk of the
destroyer *Cassin*.

Cassin (left) and *Downes* in
Drydock #1, January 1942
while being salvaged.
USN NH 54562

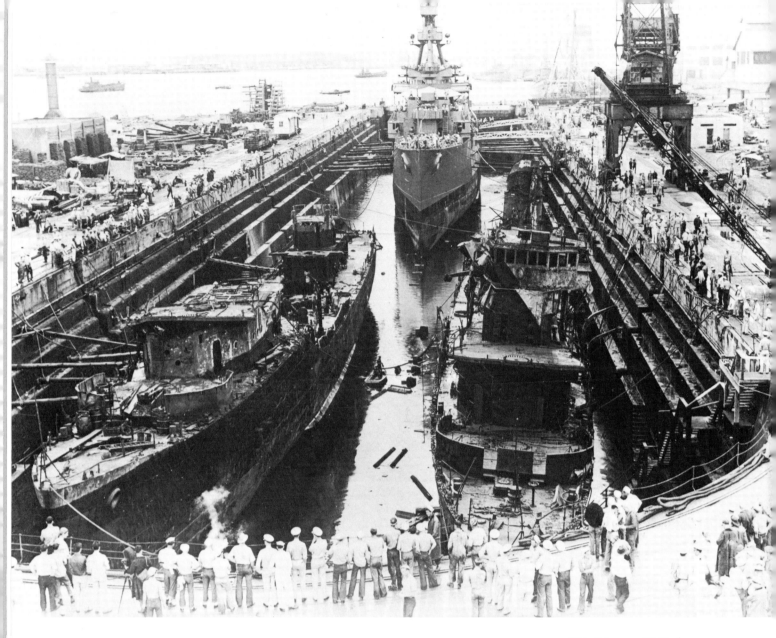

This February 1942 photo shows the *Cassin* (right) now righted, and both ships being readied for refloating. USN NH 54564

Massive damage inflicted on both destroyers in Drydock #1 is seen in this late December photo of the *Downes*. USN NH 54561

C. Emmons; and Maj. Gen. Frederick L. Martin, commander of Army Air Force Hawaii, by Maj. Gen. Clarence L. Tinker.

The smoke of battle had scarcely cleared before the first investigative board from Washington arrived in Hawaii. The Roberts Commission, headed by Supreme Court Justice Owen J. Roberts, concluded its investigation in January 1942, but the analysis of the disaster was only beginning. In the succeeding five years, seven additional boards of inquiry were convened to study every aspect of the affair. Secretary of the Navy Frank Knox had gone to Pearl Harbor almost immediately after the attack for a first-hand inspection. Before he left Washington he sent a message to all naval ships and stations:

> The enemy has struck a savage, treacherous blow. We are at war, all of us! There is no time now for disputes or delay of any kind. We must have ships and more ships, guns and more guns, men and more men—faster and faster. There is no time to lose. The Navy must lead the way. Speed up—it is your Navy and your Nation!

Admiral Kimmel and General Short were never brought to trial to defend themselves against accusations that they were negligent in their duties. Perhaps this trial would have revealed more details about how and why the American forces had been caught so completely by surprise, but the final truths about this stunning moment in history will probably remain submerged in the past, their outlines obscured by the murky waters of time.

Chaplain Howell Forgy stationed on the U.S.S. *New Orleans* during the attack uttered the phrase that would become famous during the war, "Praise the Lord and Pass the Ammunition." The phrase was spoken while he and other sailors passed anti-aircraft shells to the ship's gun deck during the attack. This phrase was also made into a popular wartime song.

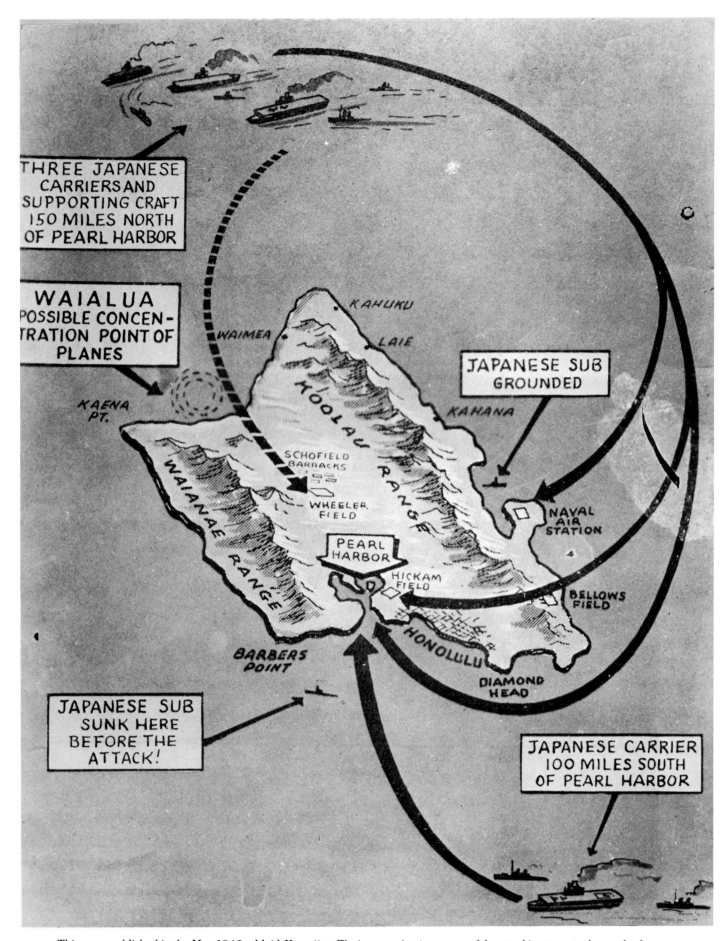

This map, published in the May 1942 tabloid *Hawaii at War* incorrectly places part of the attacking force to the south of Oahu, and errs on the route of the attacking planes. HA

Looking down Fort Street to the Aloha Tower from King Street in downtown Honolulu in March 1942. Hawaii was now under martial law. USA

Fearing food shortages for their families, housewives rushed to grocery stores on Monday morning. UH

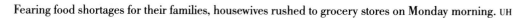

Gen. Delos Emmons, new military governor of Hawaii and commander of the Army's Hawaiian Department, leaves his headquarters just after assuming command from Gen. Walter Short on Dec. 17.
CAMERA HAWAII/WERNER STOY

Martial Law was declared in the Territory of Hawaii soon after the attack. It was not lifted until October 1944.

TERRITORY OF HAWAII

A PROCLAMATION

WHEREAS, it is provided by Section 67 of the Organic Act of the Territory of Hawaii, approved April 30, 1900, that, whenever it becomes necessary, the Governor of that territory may call upon the commander of the military forces of the United States in that territory to prevent invasion; and

WHEREAS, it is further provided by the said section that the governor may in case of invasion or imminent danger thereof, when the public safety requires it, suspend the privilege of the writ of habeas corpus and place the territory under martial law; and

WHEREAS, the armed forces of the Empire of Japan have this day attacked and invaded the shores of the Hawaiian Islands; and

WHEREAS, it has become necessary to repel such attack and invasion; and

WHEREAS, the public safety requires;

NOW, THEREFORE, I, J. B. POINDEXTER, Governor of the Territory of Hawaii, do hereby announce that, pursuant to said section, I have called upon the Commanding General, Hawaiian Department, to prevent such invasion;

And, pursuant to the same section, I do hereby suspend the privilege of the writ of habeas corpus until further notice;

And, pursuant to the same section, I do hereby place the said territory under martial law;

And I do hereby authorize and request the Commanding General, Hawaiian Department, during the present emergency and until the danger of invasion is removed, to exercise all the powers normally exercised by me as Governor;

And I do further authorize and request the said Commanding General, Hawaiian Department, and those subordinate military personnel to whom he may delegate such authority, during the present emergency and until the danger of invasion is removed, to exercise the powers normally exercised by judicial officers and employees of this territory and of the counties and cities therein, and such other and further powers as the emergency may require;

And I do require all good citizens of the United States and all other persons within the Territory of Hawaii to obey promptly and fully, in letter and in spirit, such proclamations, rules, regulations and orders, as the Commanding General, Hawaiian Department, or his subordinates, may issue during the present emergency.

IN WITNESS WHEREOF, I have hereunto set my hand and caused the seal of the Territory of Hawaii to be affixed.

DONE at Honolulu, Territory of Hawaii, this 7th day of December, 1941.

(SEAL OF THE TERRITORY OF HAWAII)

J. B. POINDEXTER,
Governor of the Territory of Hawaii.

Civilians dug air raid trenches all over Honolulu in case of further Japanese attacks. UH

Civilians, fearing another attack, built makeshift bomb shelters in their backyards. UH

Organized under fire and activated two hours after the attack, the Hawaii Territorial Guard was on duty at vital points by nightfall. UH

Sand-filled sugar sacks barricaded the telephone company entrance in downtown Honolulu. UH

Fallen sailors are honored by their comrades at Kaneohe Naval Air Station after the Pearl Harbor attack. KANEOHE MCAS

Tanks in the Honolulu streets were one sign of the military rule established after the attack. These were in front of Iolani Palace. USA

A memorial service for Pearl Harbor casualties, on Jan. 1, 1942, at Oahu Cemetery. Casualties totaled 2,388 killed and 1,178 wounded. USA

*F*ive decades have passed since the Japanese bombed Pearl Harbor, and many things have changed in Hawaii. It became the 50th state in 1959. Modern high-rise hotels, built to accommodate the postwar tourist boom, have transformed the skyline along Honolulu's Waikiki Beach.

Though they have remained a major presence, U.S. military forces on Oahu have fluctuated, in size through the years, depending on the amount of international tensions and the prevailing global strategies. The wars in Korea and Vietnam brought personnel and materiel increases, but the military presence never reached the levels it did in World War II.

Even with all the changes over the years, a serviceman going back to Oahu for the first time since 1941 will recognize most of the military installations.

Pearl Harbor Naval Base and Shipyard has changed considerably through the years to meet the needs of the modern Navy, but many of the prewar buildings are still in use.

Headquarters for 50 naval commands, Pearl Harbor is still the Navy's most important Pacific island base. More than 33,000 Navymen are stationed in Hawaii.

The airfields at Hickam and Wheeler have also changed dramatically, but many hangars, runways and other facilities are still recognizable.

Headquarters for the 15th Air Base Wing, Hickam Air Force Base supports 100 units in Hawaii and elsewhere in the Pacific, maintains aircraft repair facilities and operates the Wheeler, Bellows and Wake Island air bases. The Hickam population exceeds 11,500 active duty military and dependents, and 2,000 civilian workers.

Wheeler Air Force Base is home to the 326th Air Division, responsible for Hawaiian air defense. Fifteen other Air Force units are situated at the base, along with an Army aircraft unit.

Now an Air Force station, Bellows Field is the home of Detachment 1, 15th Air Base Wing. It serves as an antenna site for the Air Force's global radio network, a recreation area for all military services and a landing beach for Marine amphibious exercises. The old runways are still there, but are fenced off.

Haleiwa Field has been abandoned for years, its runway overgrown with weeds. As it has been since World War I, Schofield Barracks is a major base for the U.S. Army. Because many of its present facilities were built before World War II, the post looks today much as it did in 1941. It is now home of the 25th Infantry Division, including two active brigades, artillery, a support command and a reserve infantry brigade. The 45th Support Group and many of its units are also stationed there.

Abandoned for years, Ewa Marine Corps Air Station lies adjacent to the sprawling naval air station at Barbers Point. Some of its many acres of runways and parking aprons are used for a Go-kart track. More than 60 half-circle concrete revetments, built to house fighter planes, are scattered in the brush along with many delapidated Quonset huts. Some of the revetments are now used for horse stables.

Kaneohe Naval Air Station has been changed to a Marine Corps air station. It now is home of the Corps' only air-ground combat team, the First Marine Brigade.

The Marine Barracks, Hawaii—situated at Pearl Harbor—is still active and is the oldest Marine establishment in Hawaii. The second largest such facility in the Corps, it provides security for the naval installations on the island and performs ceremonial duties.

Still dotted with dozens of prewar and World War II installations, Oahu is a mecca for the military historian.

When the Arizona Memorial was dedicated in 1950, it was a temporary structure. Visitors stood on a small platform built over the sunken ship's main deck. The present memorial, rededicated in 1962 after money was authorized by Congress and raised by private subscription and donation, is a permanent monument to the approximately 900 men entombed below.

A new visitors' center operated by the National Park Service was opened in October 1980.

Monument to the dead at Kaneohe Naval Air Station (now a Marine Corps Air Station).

This spot, located across from the Marine Corps Station, Kaneohe Bay Child Care Center, is believed to be the place where the first Japanese aircraft was shot down during the attack on Oahu military bases in 1941. The plaque at the site reads "Japanese Aircraft Impact Site, Pilot-Lieutenant Iida, I.J.N., CMDR, Third Air Control Group, Dec. 7, 1941.
KANEOHE MCAS

Monument at the headquarters of the Pacific Air Forces in the old Hale Makai barracks, Hickam Air Force Base.

Fort Shafter site.

Plaque marking the site of a bomb attack at Fort Shafter.

A mock-up of a P-40 used in the movie *Tora Tora Tora* is on display at the entrance of Wheeler Air Force Base.

The headquarters building at Schofield Barracks looks today much like it did in 1941.

Palm Circle at Fort Shafter, headquarters of the U.S. Army in Hawaii and Information Center for Radar at the time of the attack.

Dock area on the northeast of Ford Island where the *Detroit, Raleigh, Utah* and *Tangier* were docked.

The morgue at the Pearl Harbor Naval Hospital was unfortunately filled on Dec. 7. More than 2,000 wounded needed attention the morning of the attack.

Building 661 and submarine escape training tank at the sub base, Pearl Harbor. Admiral Kimmel's headquarters was in this building.

The Punchbowl National Memorial of the Pacific is located in an extinct volcanic crater near downtown Honolulu. More than 18,000 war veterans, including Pearl Harbor casualties, are buried here.

Entrance to Pearl Harbor taken from Hospital Point. The submarine nets were open the morning of Dec. 7 when a midget submarine entered the harbor.

Pearl Harbor with Ford Island in the background.

Taney memorial on Honolulu's waterfront.

The U.S.C.G.C. *Taney* is the last surviving warship that was present during the attack on Pearl Harbor. It was commissioned in 1936 and berthed at Pier #6 in Honolulu Harbor at the time of the attack. She fired on attacking enemy planes. She spent the rest of the war patrolling and escorting in both the Pacific and Atlantic theatres of war. She also served during the Korean and Vietnam conflicts. She was decommissioned on Dec. 7, 1986, and is berthed in Baltimore, Md. NATIONAL PARK SERVICE

The U.S. Navy yard tug *Hoga*, built in 1940 and now called the fireboat *City of Oakland*, is typical of hundreds of World War II-era naval service craft. A well-preserved, largely unaltered example of this once-common type of craft, *City of Oakland* — ex-*Hoga* — is of exceptional significance in American history in that it is the only known surviving yard craft present at Pearl Harbor during the Japanese attack. These craft performed heroic service, extinguishing fires on burning battleships and other vessels in the harbor and rescuing wounded seamen from the oily waters of Battleship Row. *Hoga* particularly distinguished herself through her crew's actions in helping beach the burning and sinking battleship *Nevada* at Hospital Point. *Hoga* also fought fires on Battleship Row for 48 hours, particularly working on the blazing hulk of *Arizona*.
NATIONAL PARK SERVICE

World War II Japanese dive bomber leader Zenji Abe examines the remains of a "Val" dive bomber like the one he flew during his bomb run on USS *Raleigh*, Dec. 7, 1941. Photo was taken May 6, 1991, when Abe was in Fredericksburg, Texas, to participate in a Pearl Harbor 50th anniversary retrospective. This "Val" (Aichi D3A) is one of two in the United States. It was brought to the museum from Gasmata, a former Japanese airbase on New Britain Island. ADMIRAL NIMITZ MUSEUM

The *Utah* rests in the water on the west side of Ford Island. A memorial to the 58 lost sailors was dedicated in 1972.

Arizona and *Pennsylvania* Batteries

*S*ometime after the sinking of the *U.S.S. Arizona* on Dec. 7, work began to remove the huge after-turret 14-inch guns for use as coastal artillery.

Since permanent artillery emplacements were still considered to be a valuable part of coastal defense, the Army was authorized to install the *Arizona's* batteries on Oahu.

Battery *Pennsylvania* was to be placed on the tip of Mokapu Peninsula at Kaneohe Naval Air Station, to protect the eastern approaches to the island; Battery *Arizona* was to be installed on Kahe Point, to protect the southern and western approaches.

Salvaging these huge, heavy batteries and then moving them to their new sites was an enormous task, and reconstructing them was just as difficult. Large portions of the turrets had been cut away in the salvage operation. Many of the lost parts had to be built from scratch at a time when war materiel was at a premium, and many of the detailed drawings were missing.

After being placed at ground level atop large concrete casements, the turrets were to be connected to underground bunkers that would house the troops manning them.

The rebuilt turrets had to be floated on barges to beaches below the sites and hauled up specially built roads. It took more than two years to repair one of the big guns, then transport it to Mokapu Peninsula for installation as the *Pennsylvania* Battery. It was completed in August 1945 and, ironically, was test-fired on the day it became unnecessary—V-J Day. Still not completed by the end of the war in the Pacific, the Battery *Arizona* project was halted. A few years later when long-range jets and guided missiles had rendered such coastal fortifications obsolete, the massive turrets were cut up for scrap. Today the casements and underground bunkers are still intact, crumbling monuments to the old idea of fixed coastal defenses.

Remains of Penn Battery barbette on Mokapu Point. It was built to hold one of the gun turrets salvaged from the *Arizona*. The barbette is 70 feet deep with an external diameter of 50 feet and a wall thickness ranging from 9 to fifteen feet.

Above: Aerial view of *Arizona* on Sept. 25, 1942. USN *Inset:* Don Stratton of Yuma, Ariz., survivor of the *Arizona*. *Below:* A plaque was placed on the *Arizona* on Dec. 12, 1950, in memory of those who died on the ship. USN

The sunken battleship *Arizona* in 1950. A small platform on the main deck house was constructed in 1950. The present permanent memorial was dedicated in 1962. NA

The memorial to the *Arizona* and her entombed men was dedicated on Memorial Day, 1962. Construction began in 1958 after authorization by Congress and approval of President Eisenhower. The $500,000 project was designed by architect Alfres Preis.

The *Arizona* Memorial at Pearl Harbor.

D. P. JACKSON Jr	S1c	R. B. LA MAR	FC3c
R. W. JACKSON	Y3c	G. S. LAMB	CSF
J. B. JAMES	S1c	H. LANDMAN	AMM2c
E. E. JANTE	Y1c	J. J. LANDRY Jr	BKR2c
C. T. JANZ	LT	E. W. LANE	COX
E. C. JASTRZEMSKI	S1c	M. C. LANE	
V. L. JEANS	WT2c	R. C. LANGE	
K. JEFFRIES	COX	O. J. LANGENWALTER	SK3c
R. H. D. JENKINS		H. J. LANOUETTE	COX
K. M. JENSEN	EM3c	L. C. LARSON	
P. F. JOHANN		W. D. LA SALLE	S1c
D. A. JOHNSON Jr	OC3c	B. LATTIN	RM3c

		H. M. McCLUNG	ENS
		L. J. McFADDIN	Y3c
		J. O. McGLASSON	GM3c
		S. W. G. McGRADY	MATT2c
		F. R. McGUIRE	SK3c
		J. B. McHUGHES	CWT
		H. G. McINTOSH	
		R. McKINNIE	MATT2c
		M. M. MKOSKY	S1c
		J. B. McPHERSON	S1c
		I. MEANS	MATT2c
		J. M. MEARES	S2c
		J. A. MENEFEE	S1c

V. W. OGLE	
L. H. OGLESBY	
R. B. OLIVER	
E. K. OLSEN	
G. M. OLSON	
R. E. O'NEALL	
W. T. O'NEILL	
D. J. ORR	
S. J. ORZECH	
M. E. OSBORNE	
L. G. OSTRANDER	
P. D. OTT	
F. H. OWEN	
R. A. OWENS	

TO THE MEMORY OF THE GALLANT MEN HERE ENTOMBED AND THEIR SHIPMATES WHO GAVE THEIR LIVES IN ACTION ON DECEMBER 7, 1941 ON THE U.S.S. ARIZONA

THIS MEMORIAL WALL WAS INSTALLED AND REDEDICATED BY AMVETS APRIL 4, 1984

E. R. JOHNSON	MM	H. L. LEE	
J. R. JOHNSON	S1c	D. A. LEEDY	FC1c
S. C. JOHNSON	COX	J. C. LEGGETT	BM2c
S. E. JOHNSON	CDR(MC)	J. M. LEGROS	S1c
B. S. JOLLEY	S1c	M. H. LEIGH	GM3c
D. P. JONES	S1c	J. W. LEIGHT	S1c
E. E. JONES		R. L. LEOPOLD	ENS
F. B. JONES	MATT2c	S. E. LESMEISTER	EM3c
H. C. JONES	GM1c	F. LEVAR	CWT
H. JONES Jr	MATT1c	W. A. LEWIS	GM1c
H. J. JONES	S1c	N. S. LEWISON	FC3c
H. L. JONES	S1c	W. R. LIGHTFOOT	GM3c
L. JONES	S1c	G. E. LINBO	GM3c

V. G. MENO	MATT2c	T. L. OWSLEY	
S. P. MENZENSKI	COX		
H. D. MERRILL	ENS	A. P. PACE	
O. W. MILES	S1c	H. E. PARKES	
C. J. MILLER	F1c	P. J. PAROLI	
D. A. MILLER	COX	H. L. PATTERSON	
F. N. MILLER	CEM	R. PATTERSON Jr	
G. S. MILLER	S1c	H. PAULMAND	
J. D. MILLER	S1c	B. PAVINI	
J. Z. MILLER	S1c	R. P. PAWLOWSKI	
W. O. MILLER	SM1c	A. PEARCE	
W. H. MILLIGAN	S1c	N. C. PEARSON	
R. L. MIMS	S1c	R. S. PEARSON	

The *Arizona* rock on Ford Island, placed by the Navy Club of the United States of America on Dec. 7, 1955. JO2 ROB BENSON

Plaque on the *Arizona* Memorial.

The foundation for No. 3 gun turret on the *Arizona* as seen from the memorial.

Arizona remains were placed on Waipio Peninsula where they can still be found today.

ANCHOR
RAISED FROM HULK OF
U.S.S. ARIZONA
CAST IN CHESTER, PENN. 1911
WEIGHT 19,585 POUNDS

Plaque for the Anchor at the *Arizona* Memorial.

OUT OF AN HONORED PAST. . . . . .FOR A BETTER TOMORROW

U.S.S. ARIZONA MEMORIAL

A SHRINE IN THE PACIFIC WAR MEMORIAL SYSTEM
A HISTORICAL FOOTNOTE

IN 1949, THE HAWAII LEGISLATURE (ACT 288) CREATED THE PACIFIC WAR MEMORIAL COMMISSION AS THE SOLE WAR MEMORIAL AGENCY OF THE TERRITORY OF HAWAII. THE NEW COMMISSION, CONSISTING OF SEVEN MEMBERS APPOINTED BY THE GOVERNOR, WAS GIVEN POWERS TO CREATE AND MAINTAIN A PACIFIC WAR MEMORIAL SYSTEM TO HONOR THOSE WHO GAVE THEIR LIVES IN THE SERVICE OF THEIR COUNTRY.

COMMENCING 6 AUGUST 1956, THE COMMISSION UNDER THE LEADERSHIP OF CHAIRMAN H. TUCKER GRATZ, INITIATED A NATION-WIDE PUBLIC SUBSCRIPTION TO SECURE FUNDS FOR THE DEVELOPMENT AND ESTABLISHMENT OF A MEMORIAL TO THE MEMBERS OF THE ARMED FORCES OF THE UNITED STATES WHO WERE KILLED DURING THE ATTACK ON PEARL HARBOR, HAWAII, ON 7 DECEMBER 1941. AS A RESULT OF SUCH ENDEAVORS AND WITH THE AUTHORIZATION OF THE 85TH CONGRESS OF THE UNITED STATES OF AMERICA, CONSTRUCTION OF THE U.S.S. ARIZONA MEMORIAL STARTED 14 APRIL 1960. THE MEMORIAL WAS DEDICATED 30 MAY 1962.

IN 1968, THE COMMISSION, IN CONJUNCTION WITH THE UNITED STATES NAVY, COMMENCED PLANNING FOR NEW AND IMPROVED VISITOR SHORESIDE FACILITIES IN SUPPORT OF THE U.S.S. ARIZONA MEMORIAL. SPEARHEADING THIS EFFORT, THE HONORABLE SPARK M. MATSUNAGA, UNITED STATES SENATOR AND A FORMER MEMBER OF THE COMMISSION, INTRODUCED LEGISLATION FOR FUNDING TO BUILD A NEW VISITOR CENTER. AFTER PERSISTENT ATTEMPTS, WITH THE ASSISTANCE OF THE HONORABLE DANIEL K. INOUYE, UNITED STATES SENATOR, AND WITH THE SUPPORT OF THE HAWAII CONGRESSIONAL DELEGATION, THE APPROVAL FOR SUCH FUNDING WAS FINALLY OBTAINED FROM THE 95TH CONGRESS IN 1978.

THE CONGRESSIONAL APPROPRIATION TOGETHER WITH MONETARY ASSISTANCE FROM THE STATE OF HAWAII AND THE FUND-RAISING EFFORTS OF VETERANS' ORGANIZATIONS, CULMINATED IN THE COMPLETION AND DEDICATION OF THIS VISITOR CENTER 10 OCTOBER 1980. CONCURRENTLY, THE U.S.S. ARIZONA MEMORIAL AND THE NEW FACILITIES WERE PLACED UNDER THE CARE AND JURISDICTION OF THE NATIONAL PARKS SERVICE.

BY ACT OF THE 1981 STATE OF HAWAII LEGISLATURE, THE PACIFIC WAR MEMORIAL COMMISSION, HAVING SATISFIED ITS STATUTORY MANDATE, WAS ABOLISHED AND ITSELF BECAME A PART OF THE HISTORY OF THIS MEMORIAL.

IT IS HOPED THAT THE U.S.S. ARIZONA MEMORIAL COMPLEX WILL SERVE AS A MONUMENT TO ETERNAL VIGILANCE AND WILL INSPIRE THE PEOPLE OF ALL NATIONS AND THE NATIONS THEMSELVES TO JOIN HANDS AND HEARTS IN DEVOTION TO THE SUPREME IDEAL OF LASTING PEACE.

PACIFIC WAR MEMORIAL COMMISSION
DENNIS A. DAUGHERTY, CHAIRMAN
VICTORIA GUSTER, EXECUTIVE SECRETARY

1982

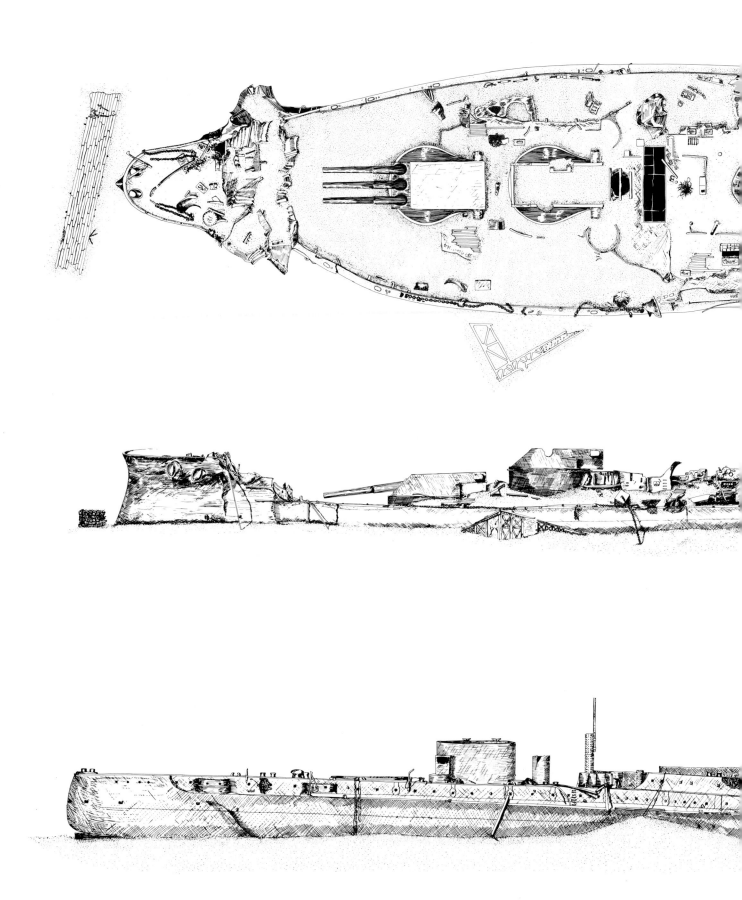

This set of drawings was developed from data obtained in the intense underwater mapping sessions that took place in 1984.

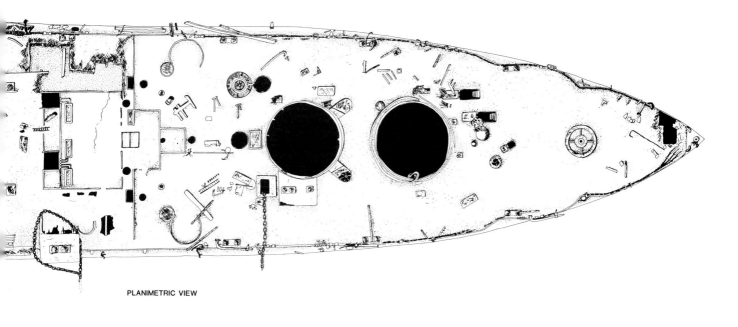

PLANIMETRIC VIEW

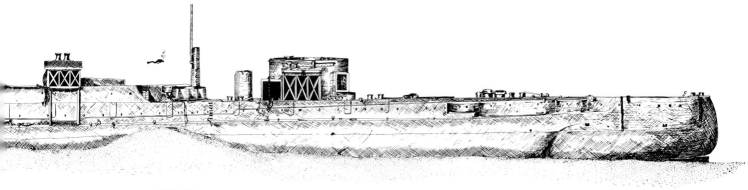

PORT ELEVATION

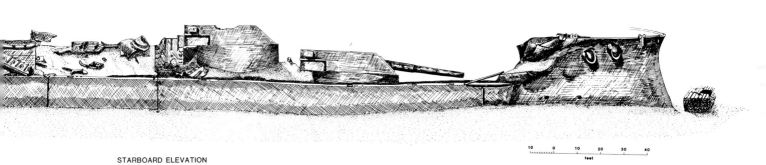

STARBOARD ELEVATION

10 0 10 20 30 40
feet

U.S.S. ARIZONA

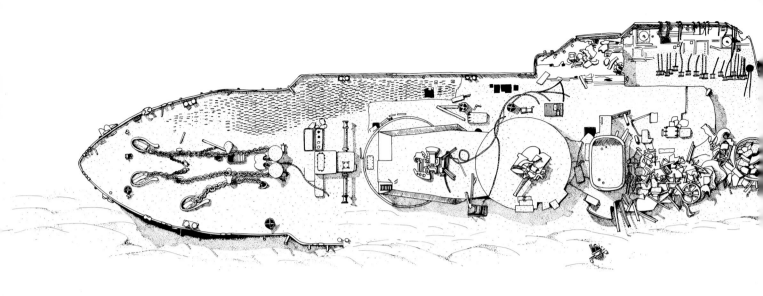

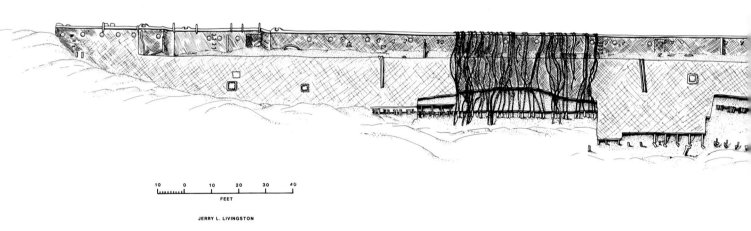

10 0 10 20 30 40
FEET

JERRY L. LIVINGSTON

Two-part drawings of remains of USS UTAH. Drawn by Jerry Livingston from underwater
operations conducted by SCRU and US Navy Reserve MDSU One (Det 319).

Oblique perspective of USS UTAH remains. Drawing by Jerry Livingston.

Underwater scenes of the *Arizona*.

The National Park Service's Submerged Cultural Resources Unit (SCRU) was given the task of mapping and photo-documenting both the *Arizona* and the *Utah* in 1984 and 1986. In 1988, underwater airplane crash sites were investigated using side-scan sonar with U.S. Navy cooperation.

Underwater measuring of the ship. After being drawn down, each feature is measured back to two points on a baseline. This allows accurate mapping through a simple geometric procedure called trilaturation.

Artifacts in ship's galley area.

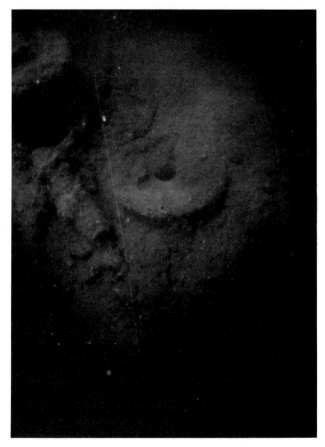

Jackstaff hole at stern, mooring bits visible to the left.

Ammunition.

Tile from galley area.

Teak decking.

An air cylinder protrudes from debris. U.S. Navy EOD divers were called in to rupture the bottle in case it was still under pressure.

Underwater scenes of the *Utah*.

Stairs lead down into the interior of the ship.

Chock on gunnel on starboard.

Pearl Harbor displays

Pearl Harbor display at the Admiral Nimitz Museum State Historical Park in Fredericksburg, Texas. The museum was established in the hometown of Adm. Chester Nimitz in 1970 by the Texas State Legislature. The museum is dedicated to everyone who served in the Pacific during World War II. ADMIRAL NIMITZ MUSEUM

A piece of the battleship *Arizona* on display at the Admiral Nimitz Museum.

Pearl Harbor display at the Intrepid Sea-Air-Space Museum on the Hudson River in New York City, N.Y. The battleship *Nevada* was used in the movie *Tora Tora Tora*.

INTREPID SEA-AIR-SPACE MUSEUM

Pearl Harbor display at Patriots Point Naval and Maritime Museum, Mount Pleasant, South Carolina.

PATRIOTS POINT NAVAL AND MARITIME MUSEUM

Cmd. Mitsuo Fuchida, commander of the Japanese air attack, is shown in this photo years after the war with former Doolittle Raider Jake DeShazer, who spent 40 months in a Japanese prison. Fuchida passed away in 1976 after suffering from old war wounds.

Japanese Torpedo Found at Pearl Harbor

by Burl Burlingame, *Honolulu Star-Bulletin*

A Japanese torpedo used in the attack 50 years ago came to the surface near Ford Island on May 2, 1991, in the jaws of a bottom-dredger clearing space for the battleship *Missouri.*

The location was off a pier built where the battleships *Maryland* and *Oklahoma* were damaged in the attack.

All ship operations in the harbor were halted when the torpedo was reported to port operations. The ferry ride to Ford Island, the path of which passes directly by the spot, was shut down, trapping people on either side.

Because of its unsafe condition, the Navy took the torpedo a mile and a half off Pearl Harbor and blew it up. A portion of it was recovered and is now in the hands of the National Park Service.

"There are very few intact artifacts from the attack," stated Bob Chenoweth, Arizona Memorial curator. "All that's usually left is bits and pieces. This one is particularly important because it is one of the two most important weapons used in the attack."

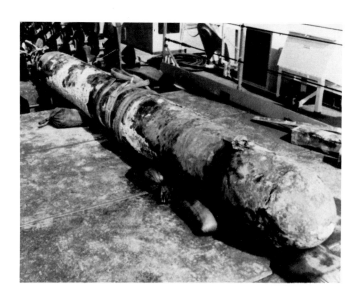

Appendix

Medal of Honor

Bennion, Mervyn, Capt., USN
Cannon, George H., First Lt., USMC
Finn, John W., Lt.(jg), USN
Flaherty, Francis C., Ens., USN
Fuqua, Samuel G., Capt., USN
Hill, Edwin J., Boatswain, USN
Jones, Herbert C., Ens., USN
Kidd, Isaac C., R. Adm., USN
Pharris, Jackson C., Gunner, USN
Reeves, Thomas J., Chief Radioman, USN
Ross, Donald K., Lt., USN
Scott, Robert R., Machinist's Mate first class, USN
Tomich, Peter, Chief Watertender, USN
Van Valkenburgh, Franklin, Capt., USN
Ward, James Richard, Seaman first class, USN
Young, Cassin, Capt., USN

Navy Cross

Austin, John A., Chief Carpenter, USN
Baker, Lionel H., Pharmacist's Mate second class, USN
Bolser, Gordon E. Lt.(jg), USN
Bothne, Adoloph M., Boatswain, USN
Burford, William P., Lt. Comdr., USN
Christopher, Harald J., Ens., USNR
Curtis, Ned B., Pharmacist's Mate second class, USN
Daly, Edward Carlyle, Coxwain, USN
Darling, Willard D., Cpl., USMC
Davis, Frederick C., Ens., USNR
Dickinson, Clarence E. Jr., Lt., USN
Douglas, C. E., Gunnery Sgt., USMC
Driskel, Joseph R., Corporal, USMC
Dunlap, Ernest H. Jr., Ens., USN
Edwards, John Perry, Ens., USNR
Etchell, George D., Shipfitter, USN
Fleming, W. D., Boatswain's Mate first class, USN
Gombasy, L. G., Seaman second class, USN
Graham, Donald A., Aviation Machinist's Mate first class, USN
Hailey, Thomas E., Sgt., USMC
Hansen, Alfred L., Chief Machinist's Mate, USN
Huttenberg, Allen J., Ens., USNR
Isquith, Solomon S., Lt. Cmdr. USN
Jewel, Jesse D., Comdr.(MC), USN

Kauffman, Draper L., Lt., USNR
Larson, Nils R., Ens., USN
Ley, F. C. Jr., Fireman second class, USNR
McMurtry, Paul J., Boatswain's Mate first class, USN
Mead, Harry R., Radioman second class, USN
Miller, Doris, Mess Attendant first class, USN
Miller, Jim D., Lt.(jg), USN
Moore, Fred K., Seaman first class, USN
Outerbridge, William W., Lt. Comdr., USN
Parker, William W., Seaman first class, USN
Peterson, Robert J., Radioman second class, USN
Pharris, Jackson C., Gunner, USN (upgraded to Medal of Honor)
Phillips, John S., Comdr. USN
Riggs, Cecil D., Lt. Comdr. (MC), USN
Robb, James W. Jr., Lt.(jg), USN
Roberts, William R., Radioman second class, USN
Ruth, Wesley H., Ens., USN
Singleton, Arnold, Ens., USN
Smith, Harold F., Boatswain's Mate second class, USN
Snyder, J. L., Yeoman first class USN
Taussig, Joseph K. Jr., Ens., USN
Taylor, Thomas H., Ens., USN
Teaff, Perry L., Ens., USN
Thatcher, Albert C., Aviation Machinists Mate second class, USN
Thomas, Francis J., Lt. Comdr., USN
Thomas, Robert E. Jr., Ens., USN
Vaeesen, John B., Fireman second class, USNR

Silver Star Medal

Kiefer, Edwin H., Lt.(jg), USNR
Marshall, Theodore W., Lt., USNR
Owen, George T., Comdr., USN
Shapley, Alan, Maj., USMC

Navy and Marine Corps Medal

Day, Francis D., Chief Watertender, USN
Schmitt, Aloysius H., Shipfitter first class, USN
Wright, Paul R., Chief Watertender, USNR

Army awards for heroism included five Distinguished Service Crosses and 65 Silver Stars.

INTELL MEMO)

         :   *INTERCEPTED BROADCAST FROM TOKYO ON BOMBING OF OAHU*

No.   10)

    The following intercepted broadcast from Tokyo, Japan, is furnished for the information and amusement of all Pilots and enlisted personnel of this Group:

RADIO TOKYO   *1740*   *JANUARY 1ST 1942*

FLIGHT COMMANDER'S REPORT ON THE GLORIOUS BOMBING OF OAHU, T.H.

EARLY THAT FATEFUL MORNING WE SIGHTED THE ISLAND OF OAHU AFTER LEAVING OUR CARRIER OUT TO SEA. CERTAIN UNITS HAD CERTAIN TASKS TO PERFORM AND IF SUCCESSFUL WE WOULD LEAVE OAHU A MASS OF SMOLDERING RUINS. OVER PEARL HARBOR WE PROCEEDED TO BOMB THE MUCH OVER-RATED AMERICAN PACIFIC FLEET. IN HARDLY NO TIME AT ALL RISING COLUMNS OF SMOKE BEGAN TO EMERGE FROM MANY SHIPS IN THE HARBOR INCLUDING A BATTLESHIP. OUR PILOTS HAD ALREADY MADE SHORT WORK OF WHEELER FIELD WHERE THE AMERICAN PURSUIT SHIPS WERE STATIONED. THEY BOMBED HANGERS AND AIRPLANES ON THE GROUND DESTROYING THEM IN GREAT NUMBERS. HANGERS WERE COMPLETELY SET AFIRE AND WERE DESTROYED DUE TO THEIR POOR CONSTRUCTION. AT NO TIME DID THE PESONNEL ATTEMPT TO FIGHT BACK DURING THE RAID. AFTER THE MAJOR OPERATIONS WERE COMPLETE, THE ANTI-AIRCRAFT BATTERIES BEGAN TO GO INTO ACTION. THEN - "I THOUGHT TO MYSELF" - "ALLRIGHT, IF YOU WANT SOME MORE I'LL GIVE IT TO YOU". WE RETURNED TO GET INTO THE FRAY ONCE MORE. THE GROUND TROOPS OBVIOUSLY BADLY FRIGHTENED DISPLAYED A POOR DEGREE OF MARKSMANSHIP AND WERE MERELY WASTING AMMUNITION. WE HAD NOTHING TO WORRY ABOUT FROM THEM. FROM AN ALTITUDE OF ABOUT 10,000 FEET WE REORGANIZED OUR DIVE BOMBERS AND WERE OFF AGAIN. "DOWN, DOWN AND DOWN WE WENT". AT 8,000 FEET WE RELEASED OUR DEADLY CARGO AND PRAYED TO OUR GUIDING FORCE THEY WOULD FIND THEIR MARK. THEN FAR BELOW US IT HAPPENED. THE HARBOR WAS A BLAZING INFERNO. WE MADE A DIRECT HIT ON A LARGE BATTLESHIP OF THE ARIZONA CLASS AND IT LITERALLY CRACKED IN HALF, SPROUTING INTO THE AIR AND DOWN AGAIN. ANOTHER LARGE WARSHIP WAS SEEN TO HAVE BEEN LISTING IN THE WATER AT A 42 DEGREE ANGLE. THE ANTI-AIRCRAFT WERE NOW BEGINNING TO GET THE RANGE AND ONE OF OUR SHIPS HAD A LARGE HOLE IN THE WING AND WE ALL PRAYED HE'D BE ABLE TO RETURN TO THE CARRIER. "BANZAI" WE ALL SHOUTED AS WE RETURNED. ANOTHER FLIGHT WAS TAKING OFF FROM THE DECK OF THE CARRIER TO COMPLETE MOPPING UP OPERATIONS. THERE WAS OAHU BEHIND US, OAHU IN FLAMES. A TASK WE THOUGHT SO GREAT THAT NONE OF US WOULD RETURN BUT ALL WE SUFFERED WAS A LARGE HOLE IN A WING TIP. THE HAND OF PROVIDENCE WAS WITH US . . .END.

Note: *It is obvious that there are several falsifications in this Flight Commander's Report, particularly the portion where the Flight Commander states the personnel made no attempt to fight back, but at the same time it must be remembered such falsifications are in keeping with established Japanese customs. They follow the German method of propaganda by "boasting and exaggerating". The record of the Pilots and ground pesonnel of this Group in fighting back on December 7th, 1941 speaks for itself, therefore it is not to be expected that an enemy such as the Japanese would admit that Pilots of our Group shot down any of their airplanes on Sunday, December 7th.*

By order of Major TYER:

FRANK E. STETSON,
1st Lieut., Air Corps,
S - 2

Yesterday, December 7, 1941--a date which will. live in infamy--the United States of America was suddenly and deliberately attacked by naval and air forces of the Empire of Japan.

The United States was at peace with that Nation and, at the solicitation of Japan, was still in conversation with its Government and its Emperor looking toward the maintenance of peace in the Pacific. Indeed, one hour after Japanese squadrons had commenced bombing in Oahu, the Japanese Ambassador to the United States and his colleague delivered to the Secretary of State a formal reply to a recent American message. While this reply stated that it seemed useless to continue the existing diplomatic negotiations, it contained no threat or hint of war or armed attack.

It will be recorded that the distance of Hawaii from Japan makes it obvious that the attack was deliberately planned many days or even weeks ago. During the intervening time the Japanese Government has deliberately sought to deceive the United States by false statements and expressions of hope for continued peace.

The attack yesterday on the Hawaiian Islands has caused severe damage to American naval and military forces. Very many American lives have been lost. In addition, American ships have been reported torpedoed on the high seas between San Francisco and Honolulu.

Yesterday the Japanese Government also launched an attack against Malaya.

Last night Japanese forces attacked Hong Kong.

Last night Japanese forces attacked Guam.

Last night Japanese forces attacked the Philippine Islands.

Last night the Japanese attacked Wake Island.

This morning the Japanese attacked Midway Island.

Japan has, therefore, undertaken a surprise offensive extending throughout the Pacific area. The facts of yesterday speak for themselves. The people of the United States have already formed their opinions; and well understand the implications to the very life and safety of our Nation.

As Commander-in-Chief of the Army and Navy I have directed that all measures be taken for our defense.

Always will we remember the character of the onslaught against us.

No matter how long it may take us to overcome this premeditated invasion, the American people in their righteous might will win through to absolute victory.

I believe I interpret the will of the Congress and of the people when I assert that we will not only defend ourselves to the uttermost but will make very certain that this form of treachery shall never endanger us again.

Hostilities exist. There is no blinking at the fact that our people, our territory, and our interests are in grave danger.

With confidence in our armed forces--with the unbounded determination of our people--we will gain the inevitable triumph--so help us God.

I ask that the Congress declare that since the unprovoked and dastardly attack by Japan on Sunday, December seventh, a state of war has existed between the United States and the Japanese Empire.

Franklin Delano Roosevelt
President of the United States

The Ad Lib

BY DAVID AIKEN

Grace G. Tully, President Roosevelt's Personal secretary, was custodian of speeches. After the speeches, the reading original was always returned to Miss Tully. With few exceptions all original speeches are at Hyde Park in the Roosevelt Library.

The famous speech on Pearl Harbor never returned to Grace. She was furious. An investigation traced it from the Capitol to the White House foyer on the hat rack to the right of the front door. Alas, poor Grace, it actually never left the Senate Chamber.

With the records of the U.S. Senate, accessioned in the National Archives, is the reading copy of the "Day of Infamy" speech. For years researchers have utilized the "Draft No. 1" with all of its marked changes without knowing if THE ad lib given in the recording of the speech was truly typed on the reading copy or if it gave the deeper thrust into the mind of the President.

Few printed texts of the speech gave THE ad lib. They usually print the handout of the speech, "The attack yesterday on the Hawaiian Islands has caused severe damage to American naval and military forces. Very many American lives have been lost."

Now that the reading copy has been accessioned, we can now begin anew our thoughts. THE ad lib was not a last minute change. THE ad lib is truly an ad lib. The President gave his heart felt regrets regarding Pearl Harbor.

He had added, "I regret to tell you that . . ." before continuing with, "many American lives have been lost." Does this mean that he truly did NOT know about Pearl Harbor?

Series of Japanese post cards issued on Dec. 8, 1942, the first anniversary of the Pearl Harbor attack.

-292-

On Dec. 7, 1942, the Japanese
government issued this com-
memorative stamp in honor of the
Pearl Harbor attack.

A Japanese propaganda post card
issued after the attack.

"REMEMBER PEARL HARBOR!"

Facts & Figures

R.C. McClay was a navy ensign on lookout duty on the U.S.S. *Condor* the morning of Dec. 7. He spotted the conning tower of the midget sub that was sunk at the harbor's entrance by the U.S.S. *Ward*. McClay was thus the first American to sight the enemy the morning of the attack.

G.A. Myers was a Seaman 2nd Class on the submarine U.S.S. *Cachalot* berthed at 1010 Dock. He was the first submariner to die in the war.

Frank Knox (1874-1944) was Secretary of the Navy at the time of the attack. He was a "Rough Rider" during the Spanish-American War and served in World War One. His daughter Elyse was a movie actress and married football star Tom Harmon.

Joseph Grew (1877-1965) was the United States Ambassador to Japan at the time of the attack. He had previously served in Germany and the Austrio-Hungarian Empire during the early days of World War One. His wife was the granddaughter of Commodore Matthew C. Perry who opened Japan to the outside world in the 1850s. After he was repatriated in 1942. Grew became undersecretary of state.

Annie G. Fox, a nurse at Hickam Field, was the first woman to receive a Purple Heart, not for wounds but for bravery.

Tadao Fuchikami was the RCA messenger who delivered a message from Gen. George C. Marshall to Gen. Walter Short advising him that after an ultimatum delivered to the United States government on Dec. 7, an attack was possible. Unfortunately the message was delivered while the "possible" attack was in progress.

George Cannon was a Marine Corps lieutenant stationed on Sand Island of the Midway Islands on Dec. 7. He was the first Marine to be awarded the Medal of Honor. He was a battery commander of a coastal battery when mortally wounded by a bomb from an attacking Japanese plane the night of Dec. 7. He refused to be evacuated until his men were cared for.

Edgar Rice Burroughs, the creator of the famous character "Tarzan" was a civilian in Hawaii at the time of the attack. He helped dig trenches on the beaches after the attack. He served as a news correspondent during the war.

Ship Losses:

Ninety-six ships were at Pearl Harbor on Dec. 7, 1941. Of these 19 were sunk or seriously damaged.

BATTLESHIPS:
Arizona — sunk, total loss.
Oklahoma — sunk, total loss.
West Virginia — sunk, later raised and repaired.
California — sunk, later raised and repaired.
Nevada — beached, heavily damaged, repaired.
Pennsylvania — minor damage, repaired.
Maryland — minor damage, repaired.
Tennessee — minor damage, repaired.

TARGET SHIP:
Utah — sunk, total loss.

LIGHT CRUISERS:
Helena — damaged, repaired.
Honolulu — damaged, repaired.
Raleigh — damaged, repaired.

DESTROYERS:
Cassin — damaged beyond repair.
Downes — damaged beyond repair.
Shaw — severely damaged, repair.

OTHER SHIPS:
Oglala (minelayer) — sunk, salvaged and repaired.
Curtiss (seaplane tender) — severely damaged, repaired.
Vestal (repair ship) — severely damaged, repaired.
Sotoyomo (tug) — sunk, salvaged and repaired.

Aircraft Losses:
U.S. NAVY — 92 lost, 31 damaged.
U.S. ARMY — 96 lost, 128 damaged.
JAPANESE — 9 fighters, 15 dive bombers, 5 torpedo bombers.

Pearl Harbor Movies

The Japanese movie *I Bombed Pearl Harbor* was produced by Toho Ltd. and released in the United States in November 1961. It is a fictionalized account of a Japanese navigator who attacked Pearl Harbor and survived the Battle of Midway. It was produced by Tom Oyaki Tanaka and directed by Shue Matsubayashi.

From Here To Eternity, adapted from James Jones's novel, was released by Columbia Pictures in September 1953. It starred Burt Lancaster, Frank Sinatra, Montgomery Clift, Deborah Kerr, Donna Reed, Phil Ober, Mike Shaughnessy, Jack Warden and Ernest Borgnine. The movie was nominated for 13 Academy Awards and received eight. Sinatra received the best supporting actor award and Reed the best supporting actress award.

The *Final Countdown* was released by United Artists in 1980. It starred Kirk Douglas, Martin Sheen, Katherine Ross, James Farentino and Charles Durning. The movie concerns an American aircraft carrier in 1980 caught in a time-warp that takes it back to Dec. 7, 1941. It was filmed on the USS *Nimitz* in Norfolk, Va., and at Key West, Fla.

Tora! Tora! Tora!

For several years, there was great skepticism within both American and Japanese film circles about the making of *Tora! Tora! Tora!*. Yet, by the summer of 1968, both governments looked favorably on the re-telling of these dramatic events and moments in history. Bitter enemies no longer, but rather allies in an uncertain world, they agreed that the monumental story of both sides should be told—that it contained lessons for the future.

Perhaps Minoru Genda, the Japanese naval strategist who was given the assignment of planning the raid, summed it up best: "I would hope that we have all reached a level of intelligence, and understanding, where nations can treat history as it happened." So, after months of international negotiation, the Japanese motion picture industry joined with the American film establishment to launch what was to be a precedent-setting venture—one of the largest ever mounted, and certainly one of the most unusual.

There were two separate films to be made, one by the Japanese production unit, to be filmed in Japan with Japanese technicians and a Japanese cast, the other, by American technicians with an American cast. Once completed, these two films would be edited into a single three-hour roadshow motion picture.

Again, experienced production personnel on both sides of the Pacific viewed the project skeptically. Simultaneous filming by two separate and distinct companies on one story! Separated by thousands of miles! The great barrier of language! Different production methods! Different equipment!

Yet the importance of the film story would surpass any predicted difficulties. The one common denominator was the medium: film. The singular and overriding goal on both sides was to get the "film into the can." And not unexpectedly, the solution to creative communication between Japan and America in the making of *Tora! Tora! Tora!* turned out to be visuals—661 sketches representing scenes to be shot by each side.

For everyone involved, this was a pathfinder operation, a first in film history. It proved quite elegantly that the "impossible" was not impossible at all.

20th Century Fox

The battleship *Nagato*, 660 feet in length, was reconstructed of wood from the original plans. It was the largest film set ever built in Japan and was used for filming for seven weeks.

OTTO LANG

Another set was constructed of the *Akagi*'s hangar deck. Both sets were constructed at Ashuyu on the island of Kyushu.

The Pearl Harbor History Association, Inc., is a nonprofit corporation chartered by the Commonwealth of Virginia. Its purpose is to conduct research on the Pacific War and to provide educational information to all citizens. The organization has no interest in political activity or in furthering any cause, other than the records of the Pacific War, and Pearl Harbor in particular.

About the Author

Stan Cohen is a native of West Virginia and now resides in Missoula, Montana. He was only three years old at the time of the attack, yet has had an interest in Pearl Harbor and the Pacific War since he was old enough to read. After spending many years as a geologist, ski area manager and historical park director, he established Pictorial Histories Publ. Co. in 1976. Since that time, he has authored or co-authored 69 books and published over 275. He has traveled to many Pacific battlefields, and has interviewed many Pearl Harbor survivors at their reunions.

About the Contributors

Ernest Arroyo, a resident of Stratford, Conn., is a production manager for a printing firm. He has been a student of U.S. Naval history for over 35 years. He maintains a large collection of U.S. Navy ships and a reference library. He has contributed photos and data for over a dozen books on naval and maritime subjects. He is currently Vice-President of Pearl Harbor History Associates, Inc.

Robert D. Bracci, the creator of the highly detailed scale diorama of the Pearl Harbor naval base, has been researching the Japanese attack as well as the physical layout of the harbor and its surrounding land facilities as it existed in December of 1941 since he was a young high school student. He began actual construction on the project nearly 30 years ago after studying ships location charts of Pearl on December 7th. This appropriately titled piece, "Sunrise on the Fleet—0755 Hrs., December 7, 1941—The Final Moment of Peace" (copyright 1991), is the culmination of nearly 20,000 hours of labor and research. The three-dimensional geographical replica encompasses a scale nine-square-mile area of the tropical anchorage, condensed within a four-foot-square miniature display format. An award-winning model builder since his youth, his miniature vignettes and dioramas of 20th century military subjects have been displayed in schools, libraries and galleries as well as model conventions. He has been a member of the International Plastic Modelers Society since '74 as well as the Pearl Harbor History Associates, Inc., since '87. A native of Connecticut, he holds a degree in history (BA '69) as well as a degree in graduate studies (MPA '81). He served with the U.S. Army's 1st Air Cav Div. in Vietnam, 1969-71. Bob has worked in the field of law enforcement for the past 18 years.

David W. Aiken has been a contract illustrator for over 25 years. His work has been in color and industrial research, development, publications, photography and museology. His hobby is mineralogy.

Aiken has been a student of World War II for 35 years. In 1961, his study of Pearl Harbor began a deeper search of the Pacific War. Air Force duty at Hickam AFB, Hawaii, in 1966-67 guided his attention directly upon Pearl Harbor's American and Japanese missing in action airmen. He is a Pearl Harbor History Associates director.

His data base on Japanese aviation is utilized by many researchers, artists, authors, historians, museums and miniature builders. His personal interest is the Doolittle Raid, American aerial defense of New Guinea, the 49th and 475th Fighter Groups, the 100th Bomb Group (ETO) and MIA aircraft recovery.

Paul Bender is a marine artist with a strong interest in naval ships and aircraft of World War II. A member of the American Society of Marine Artists, Mr. Bender has supplied illustrations for other Pictorial Histories publications, as well as artwork for the Conway Maritime Press, United States Naval Institute Press and Newsweek magazine.

About the Cover Artist

Mel Brown resides in Austin, Texas, with his wife and three children. He is a self-taught artist specializing in aviation and landscapes. Brown is a member of the American Society of Aviation Artists and a contributor to the prestigious USAF Art Collection. His lifelong fascination with aircraft is due in large part to being born and raised in San Antonio, Texas, home to four Air Force Bases and having a father in the USAF.

World War II is Brown's main area of interest and in this respect he considers his artwork to be of an historical nature rather than merely depictive. He has traveled in England and Germany to do research and also has an extensive personal library. Brown is an accomplished modeler and often builds highly detailed plastic models before beginning a painting of the subject. This attention to detail has brought him important commissions, including paintings now hanging in the U.S. Air Force Academy, the Air University at Maxwell Air Force Base and in private collections both here and abroad.